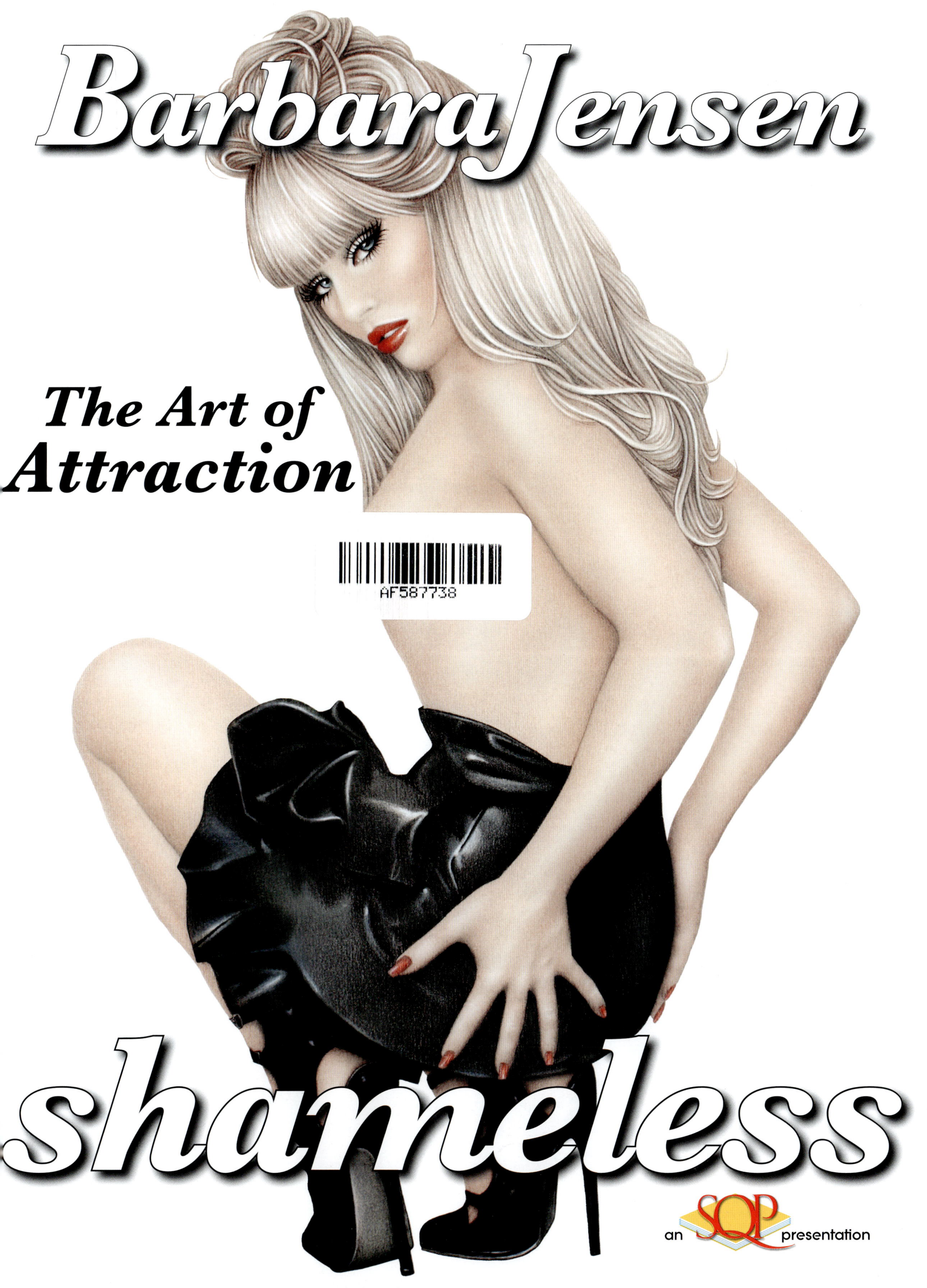

Barbara Jensen
The Art of Attraction
AF587738
shameless
an SQP presentation

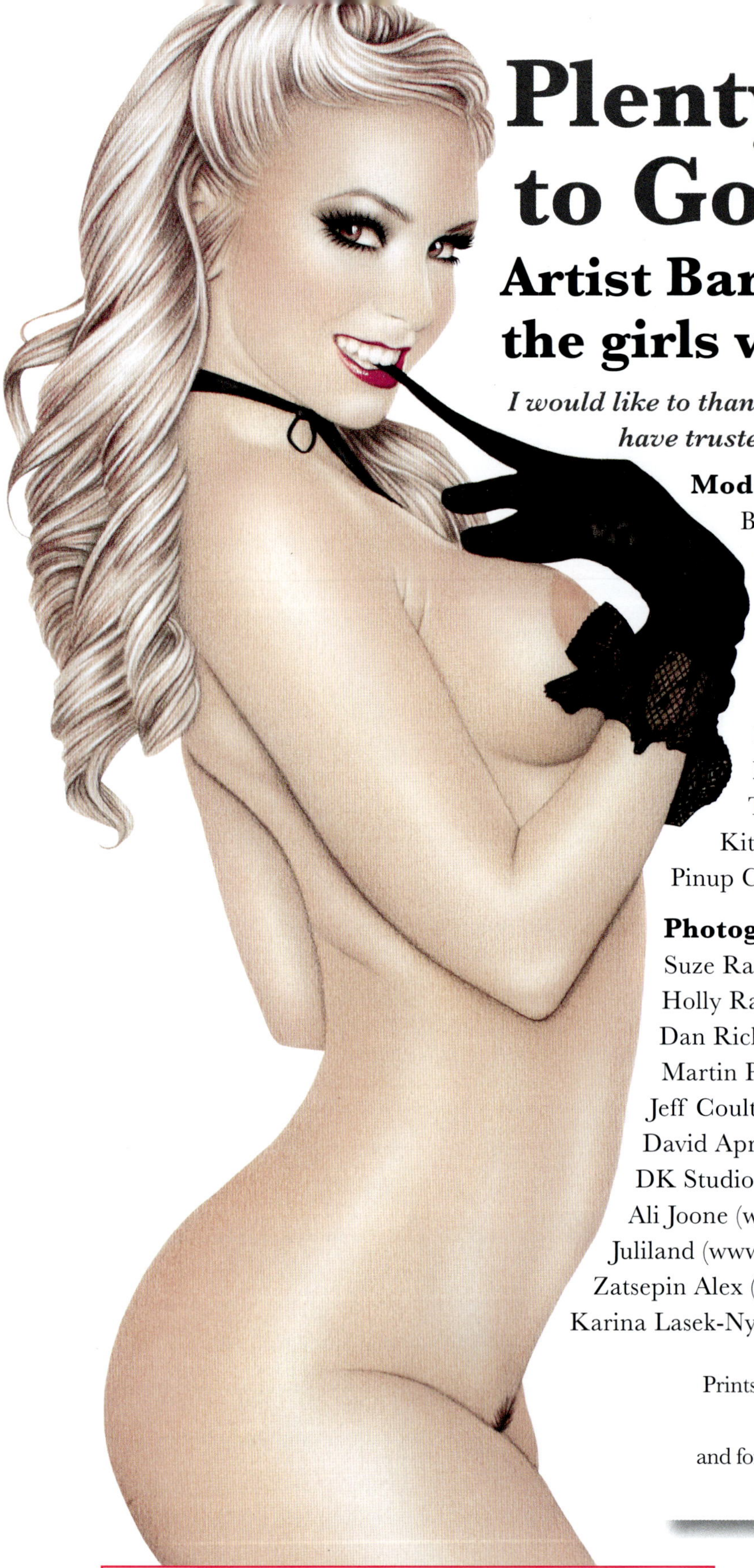

Plenty of "*Shame*" to Go Around...

Artist Barbara Jensen just *loves* the girls who love to *tease*...

I would like to thank all of the models and photographers who have trusted me with their work

Models:
Bianca Beauchamp (www.biancabeauchamp.com)
Miss Mosh (www.themoshroom.com)
Zdenka Podkapova (www.sexy-zdenka.com)
Kayden Kross (www.clubkayden.com)
Liz Ashley (www.thelizashley.com)
Michelle Thorne (www.michellethorne.com)
Elisanth (www.elisanth.com)
Michelle Thorne (www.Michellethrone.com)
Tanit Isis (www.tanit-isis.deviantart.com)
Kity Young, SINderella Rockafella, Alexandra Rose,
Pinup Candy, Tancy Marie, Jesse Jane, Valerie Virgin, Nikki Masters

Photographers:
Suze Randall (www.suze.net)
Holly Randall (www.hollyrandall.com)
Dan Richards (http://d2L2.deviantart.com)
Martin Perreault (www.marticperreault.com)
Jeff Coulter (www.visualpoison.com)
David April (http://dsa157.deviantart.com)
DK Studio (www.dk-studio.com)
Ali Joone (www.facebook.com/alijoone)
Juliland (www.juiland.com)
Zatsepin Alex (www.facebook.com/Zatsepin.Alex)
Karina Lasek-Nylonessa

Would you like to commission your very own piece of Jensen art? Contact her directly at Arteest111@aol.com

Prints and galleries of Barbara's work can be found at
www.Eroticartistgallery.com
and for the psp graphics world her tubes can be found at
www.Barbarajensentubes.com

Barbara Jensen's Shameless
The Art of Attraction

Book design by Grassy Knoll Studios.

Published by SQP Inc.
PO Box 248 - Columbus NJ 08022

Sal Quartuccio & Bob Keenan - Publishers

For a free, full color catalog showcasing the entire SQP line of erotic, fantasy, and pin-up artwork, go to:
www.sqpartbooks.com

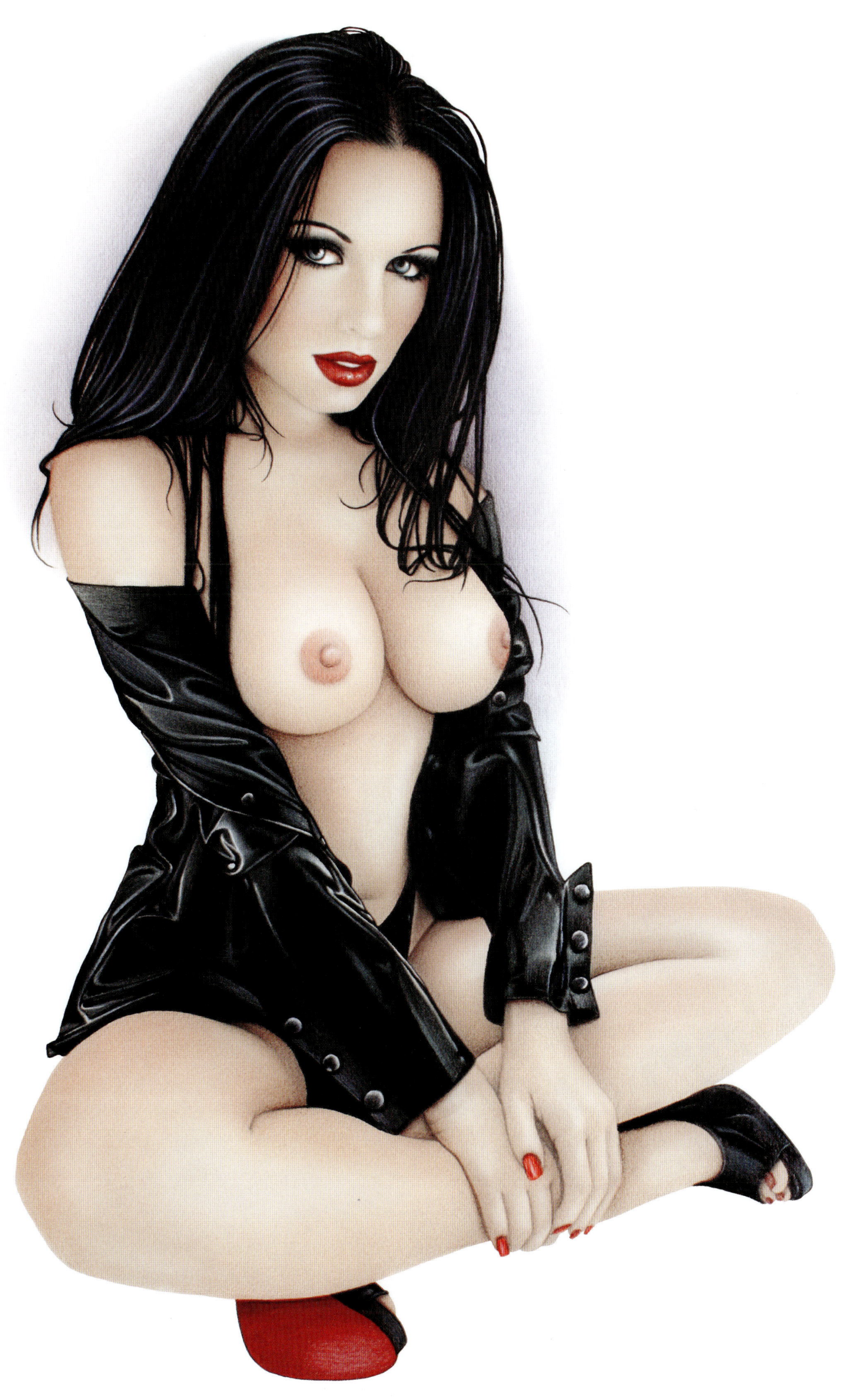

Blackberry

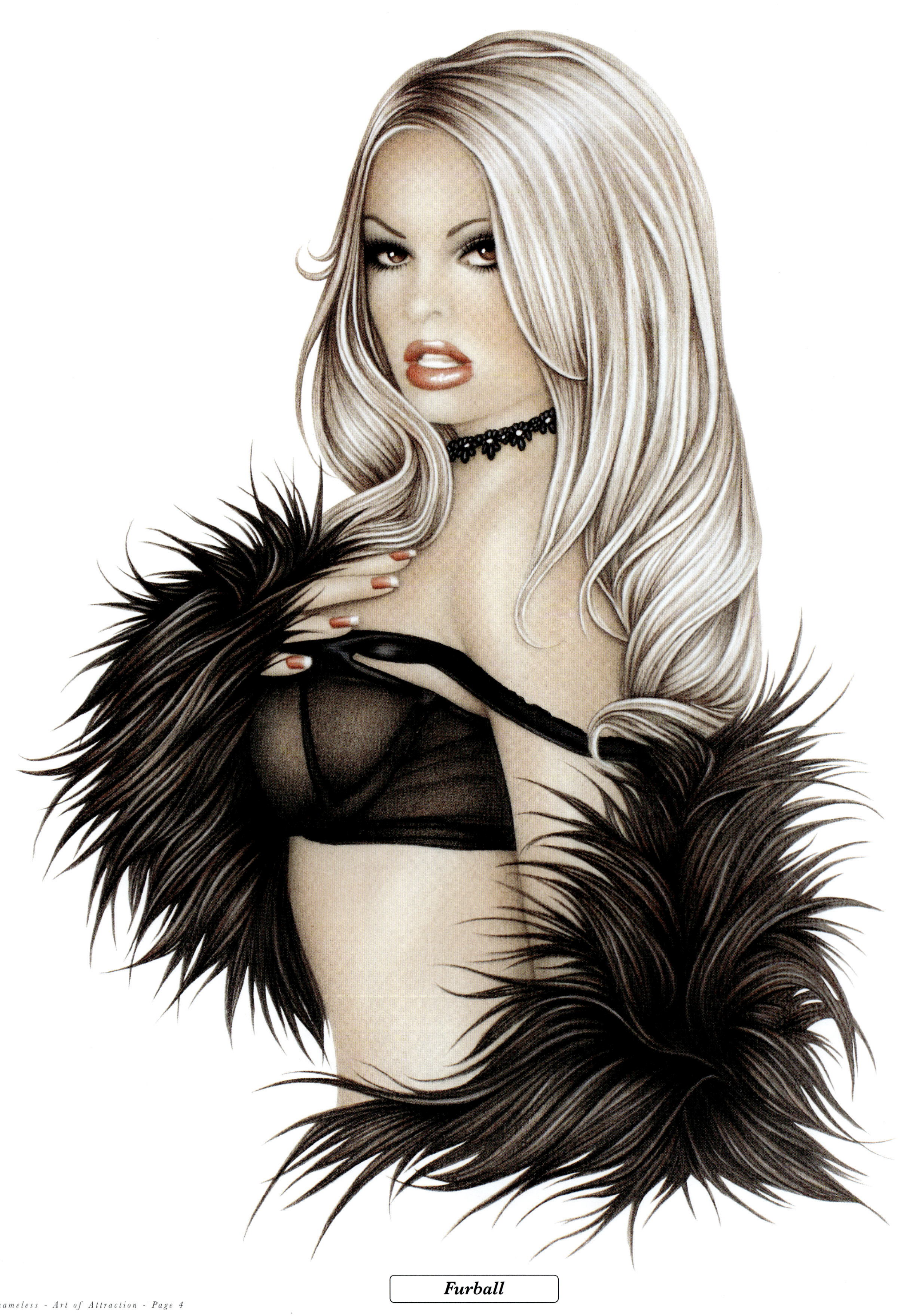

Furball

Unseamly

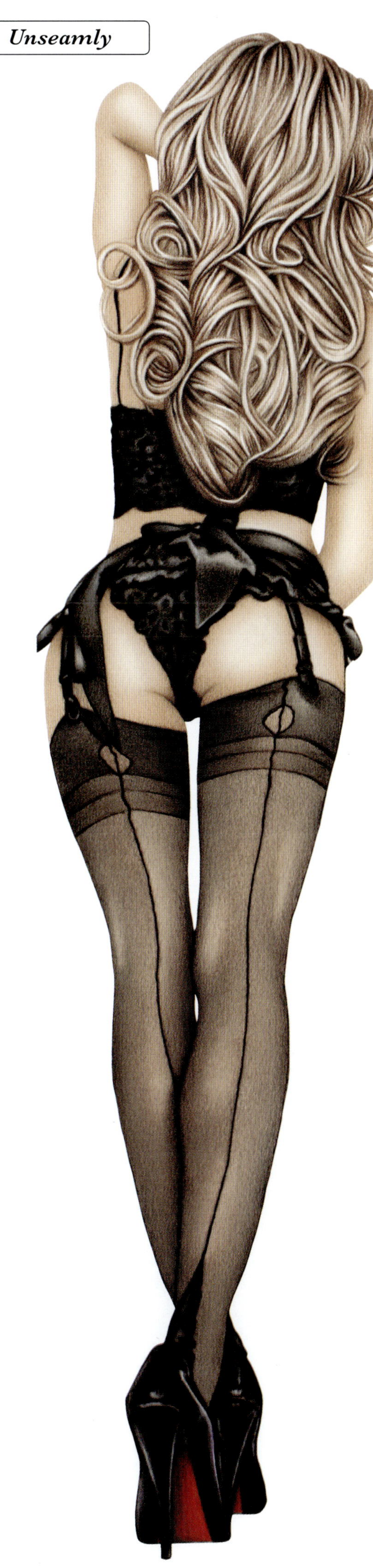

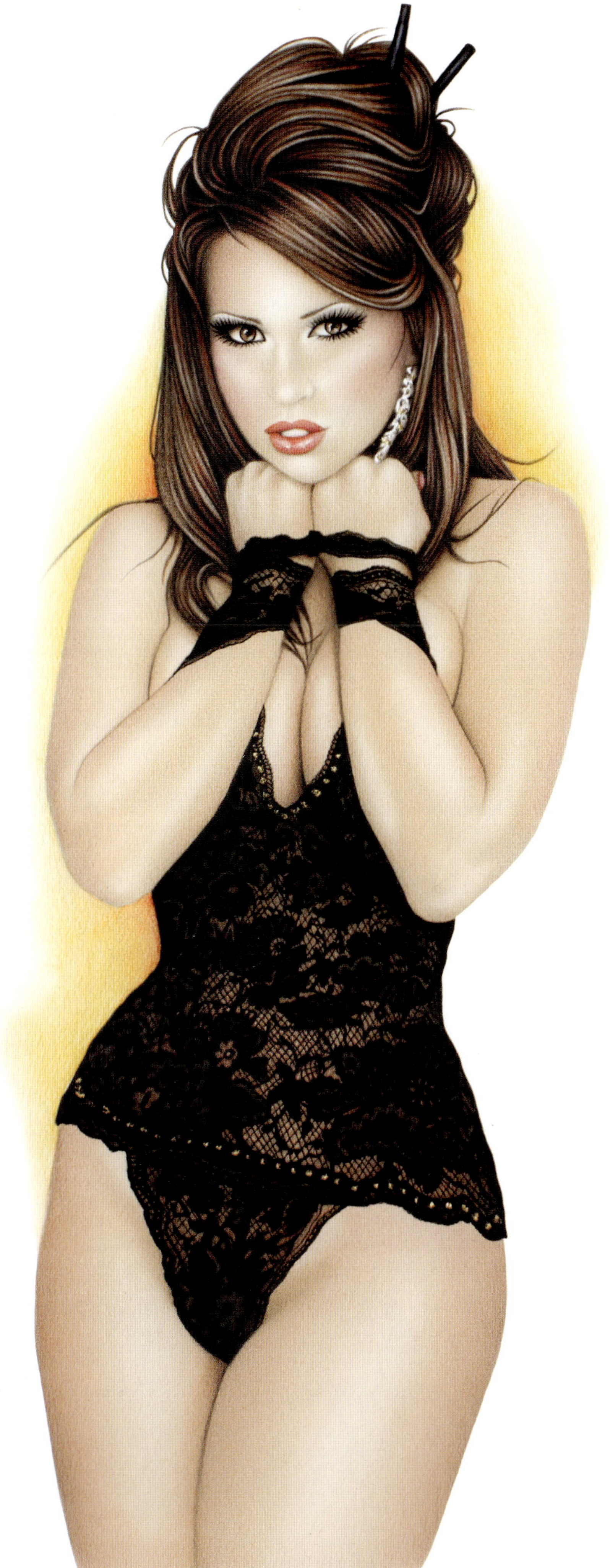

Bashful

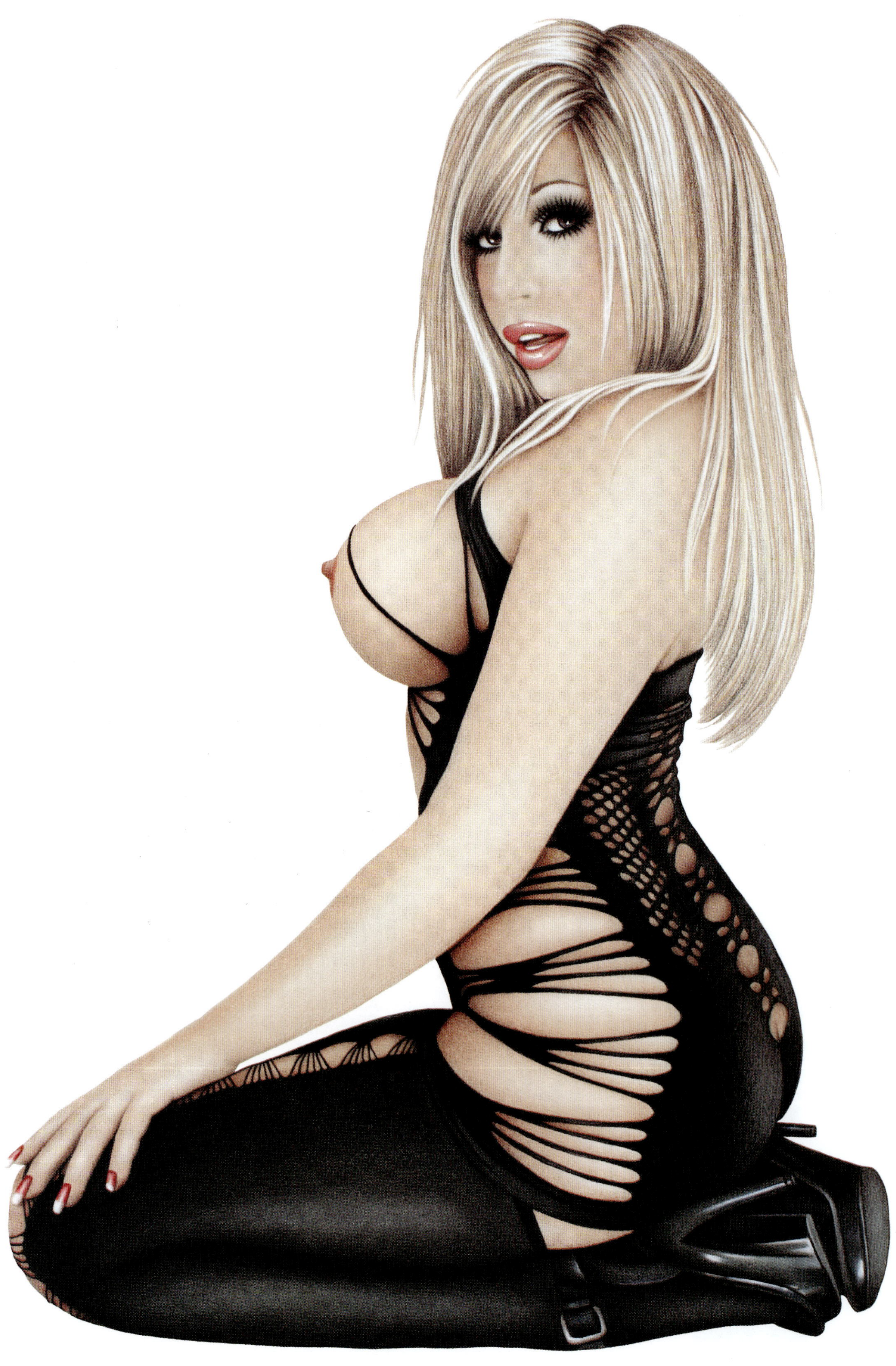

Perk Me Up

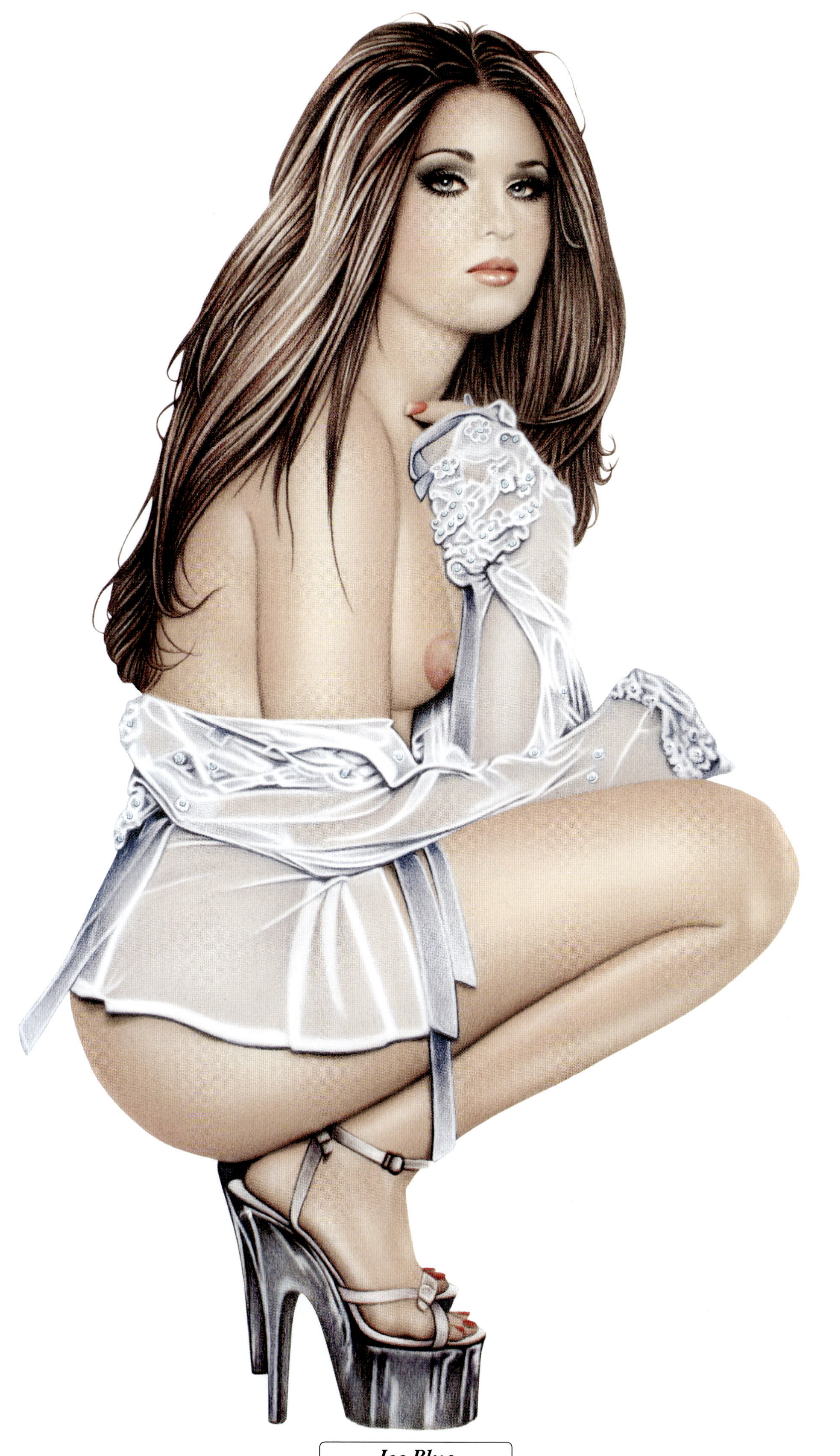

Ice Blue

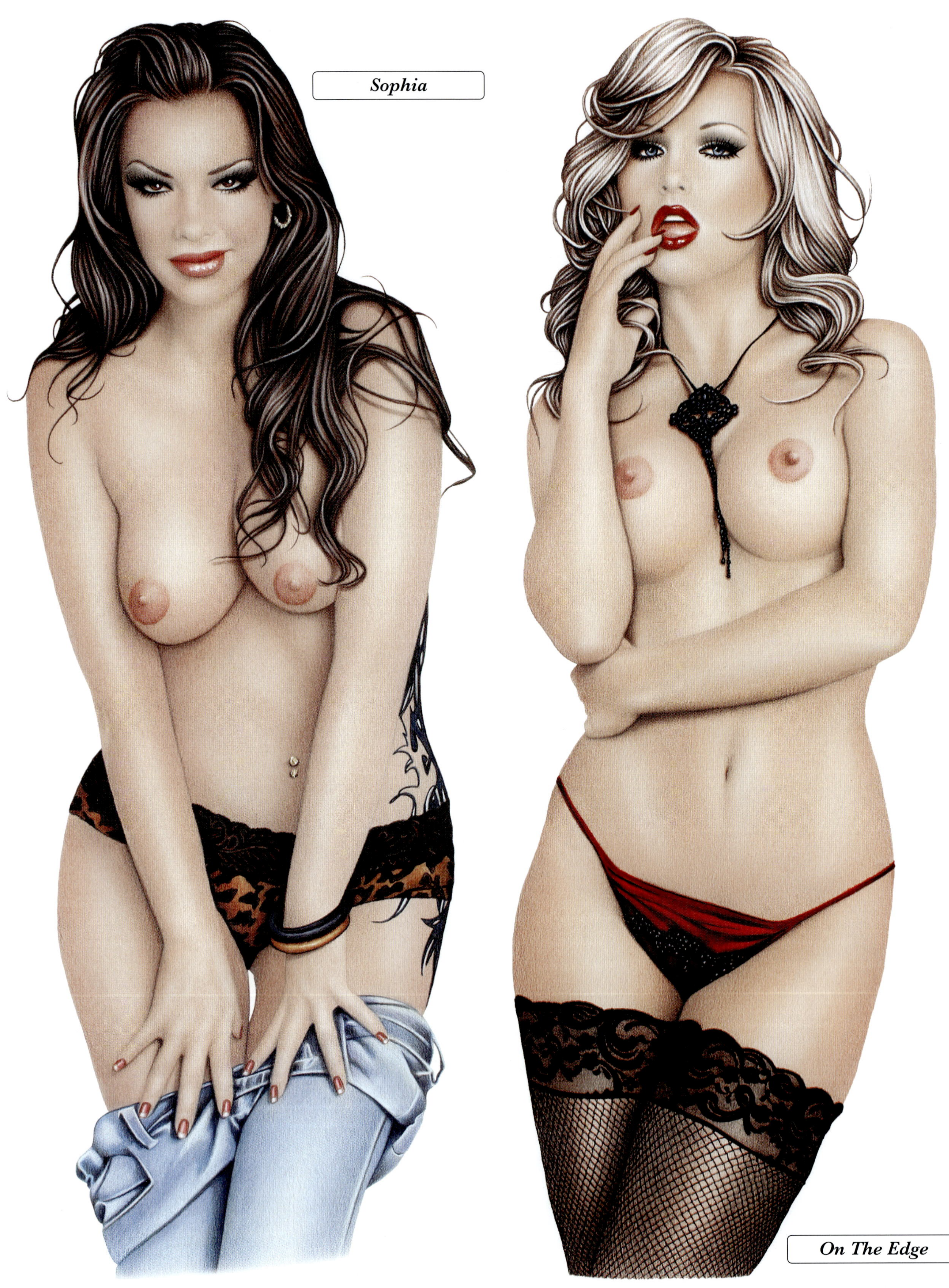

Sophia

On The Edge

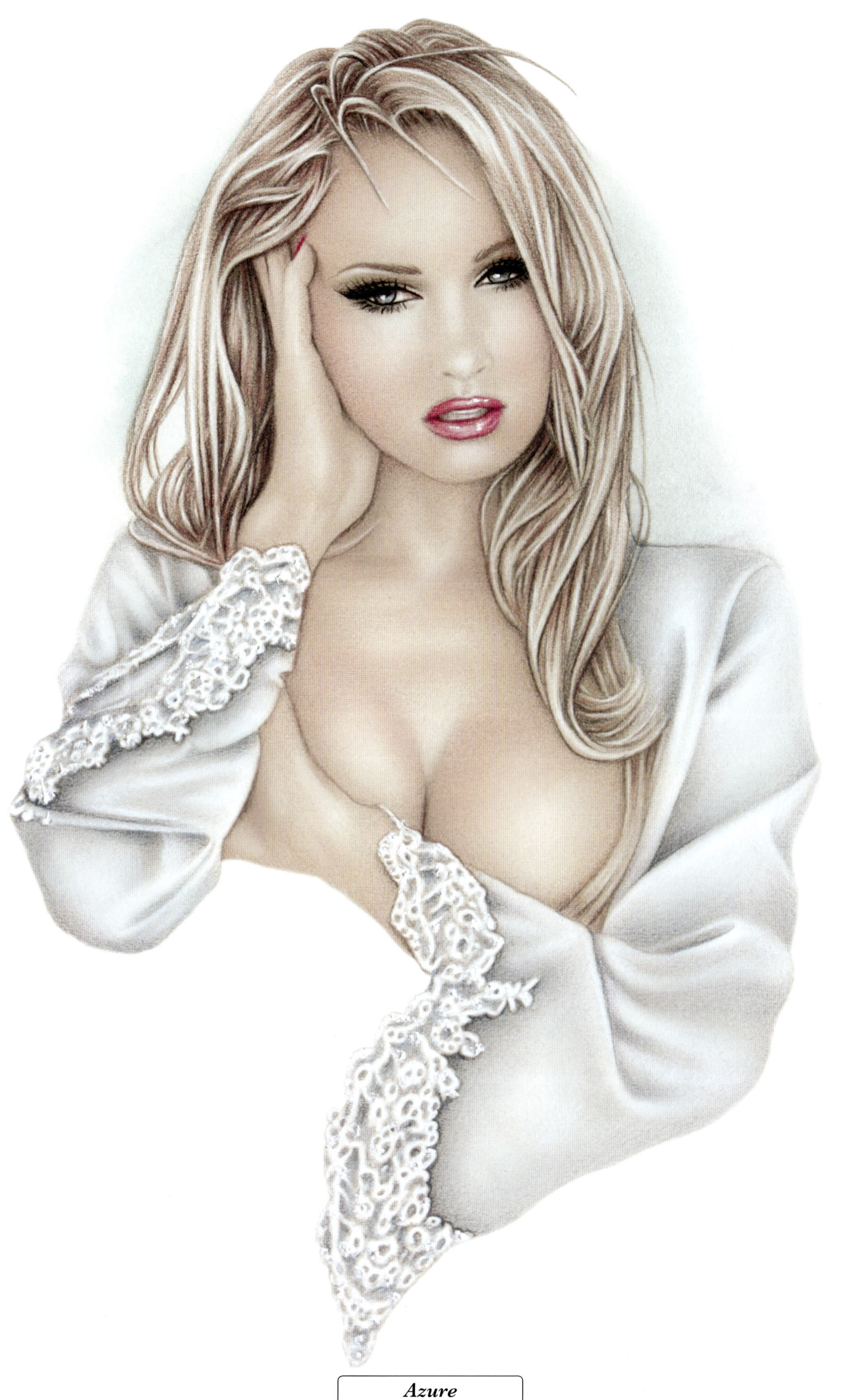

Azure

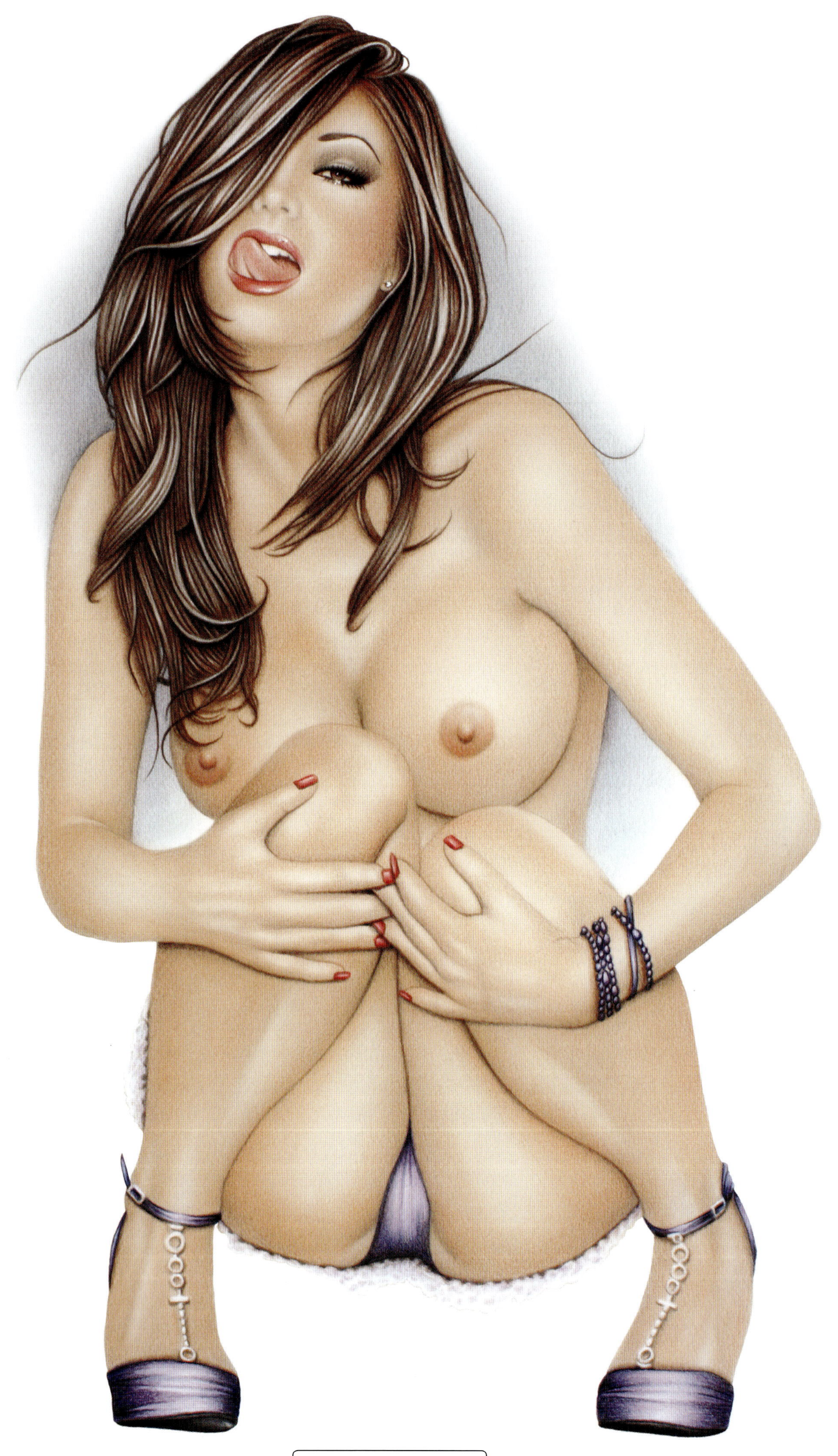

Tongue Twister

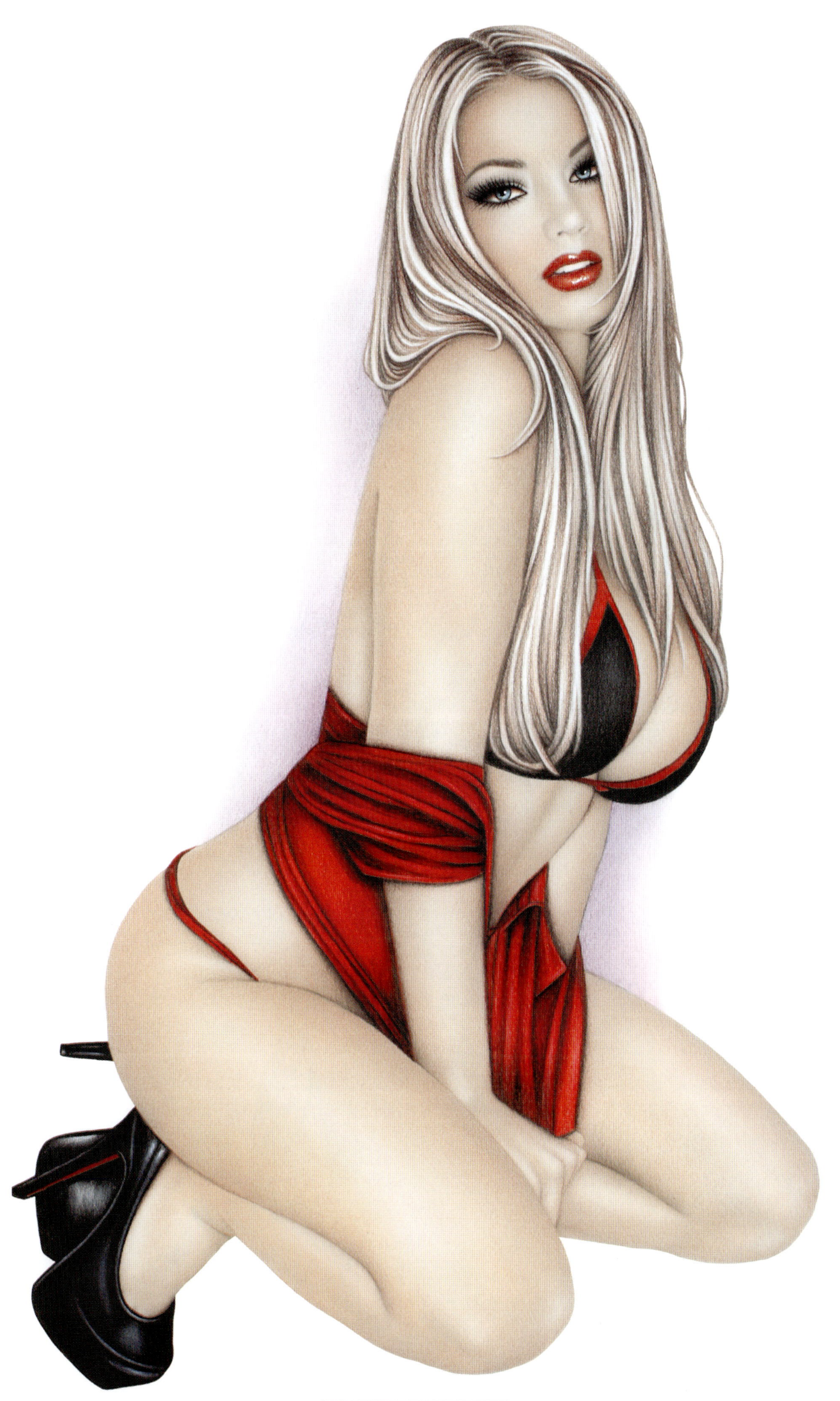

Raspberry Tart

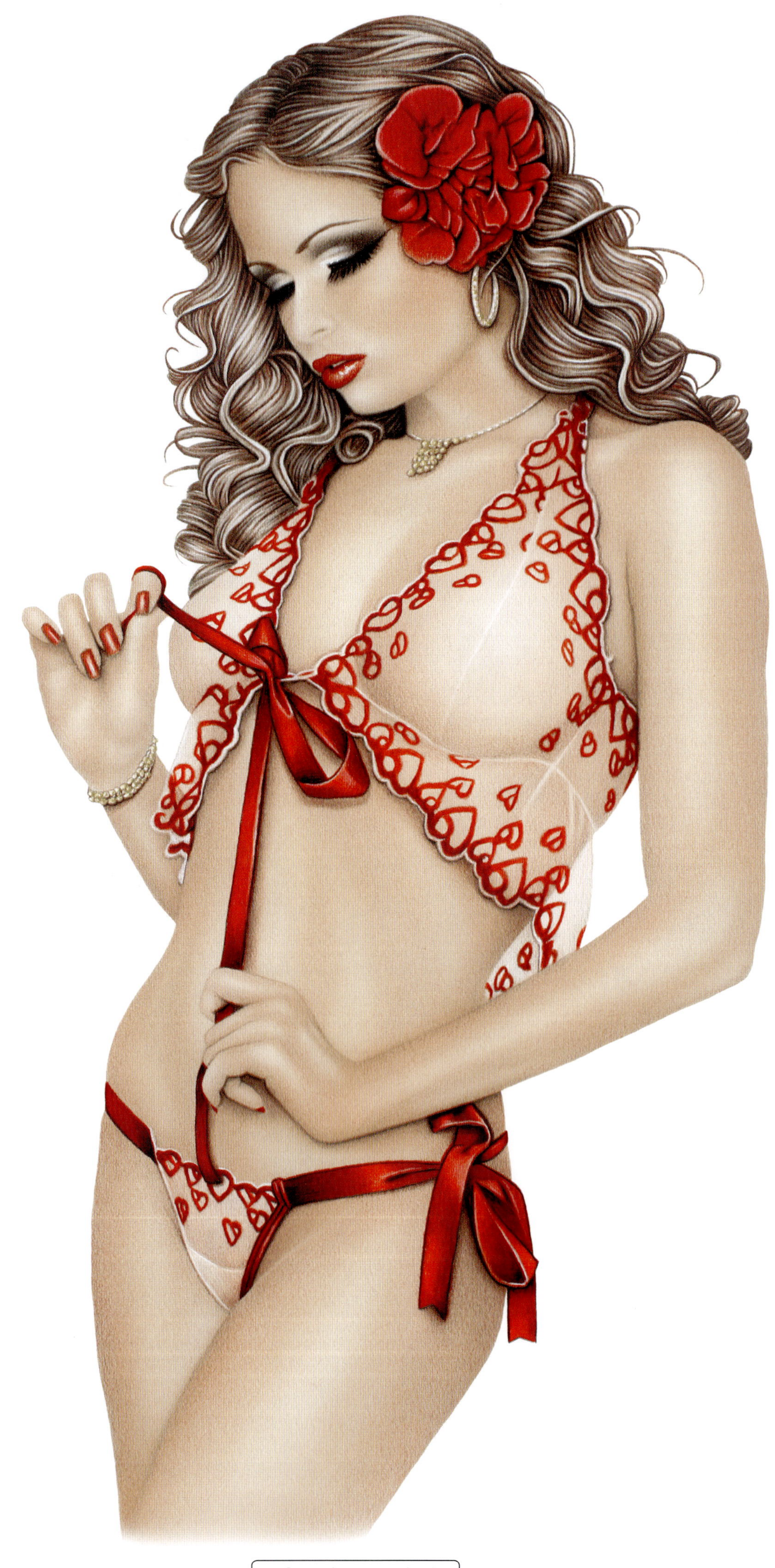

Coming Untied

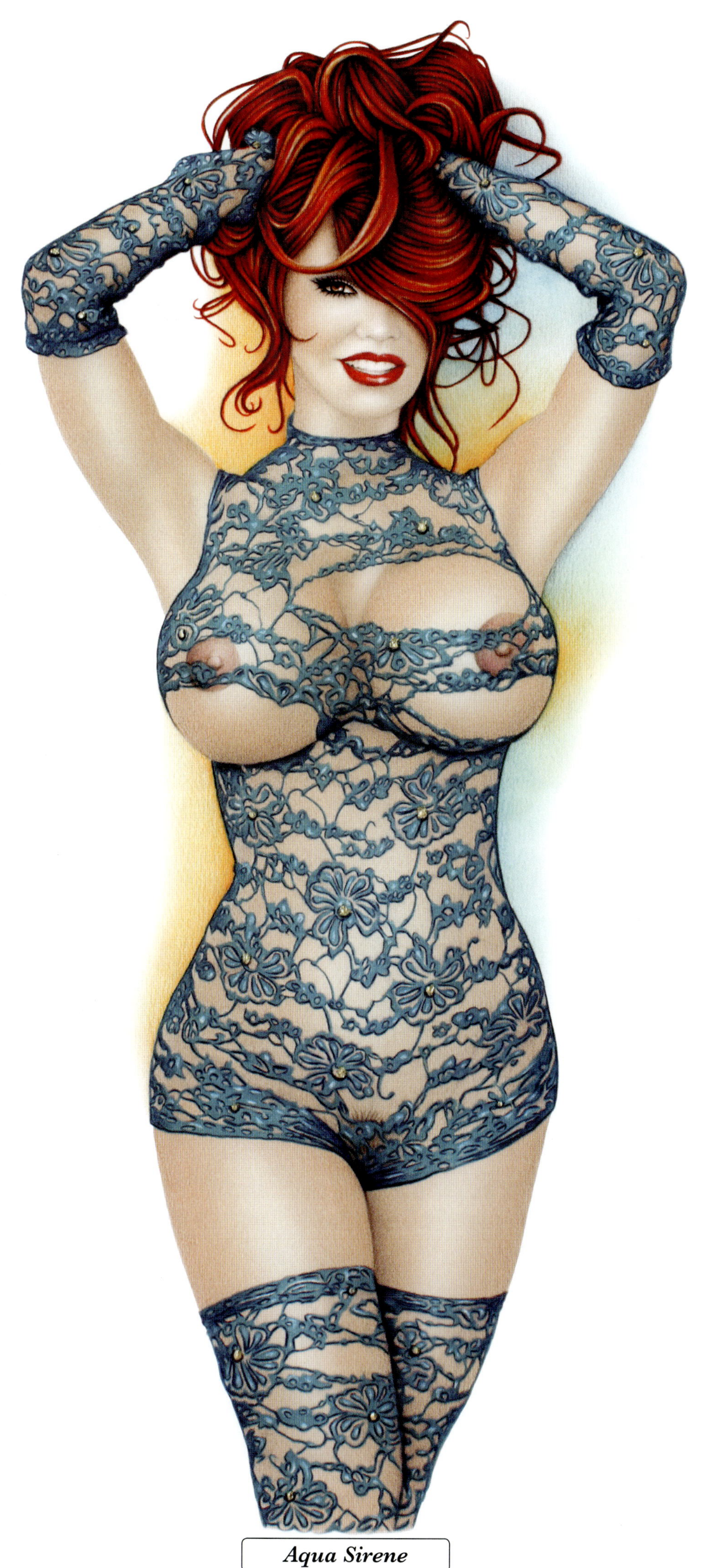

Aqua Sirene

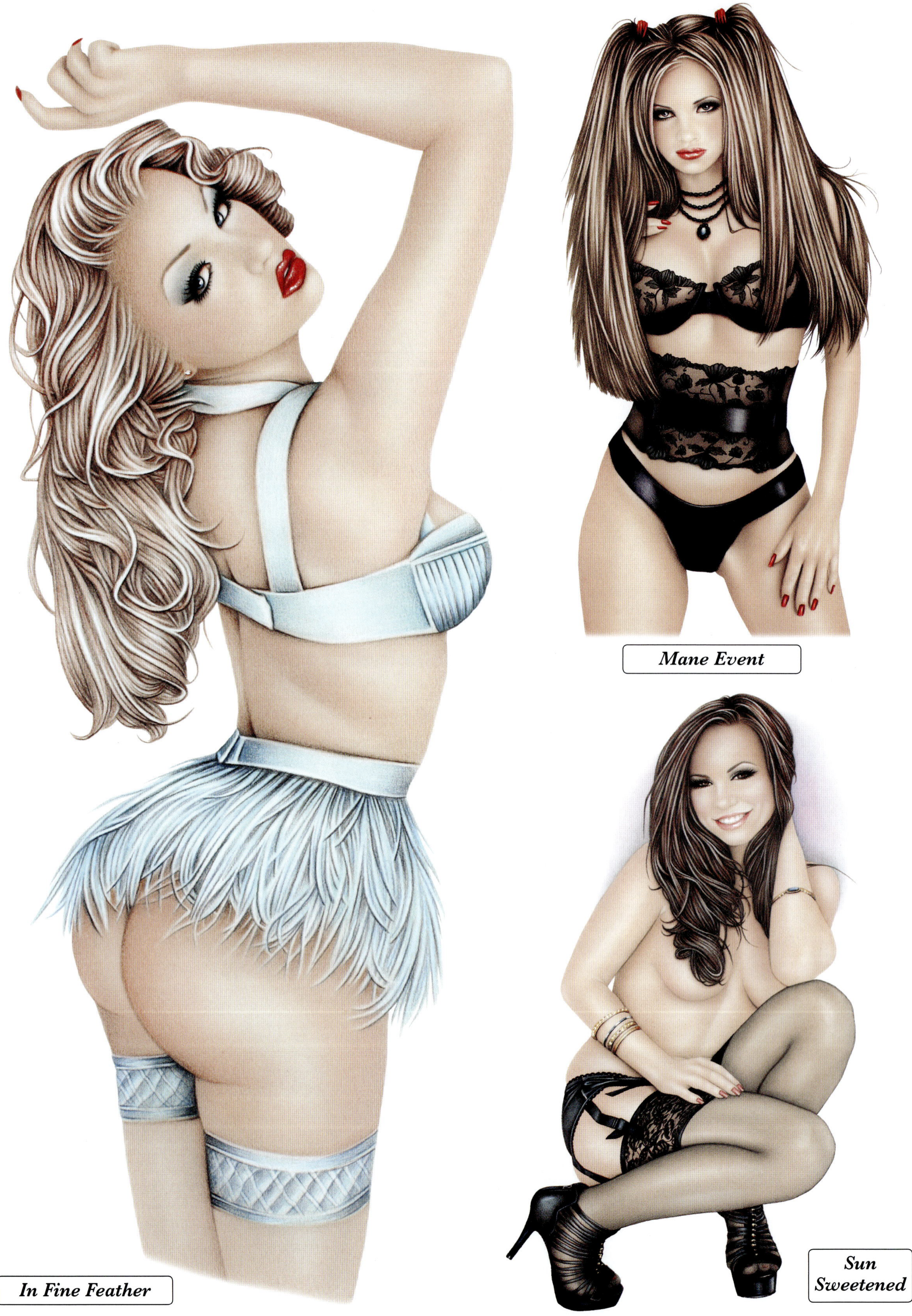

Mane Event

Sun Sweetened

In Fine Feather

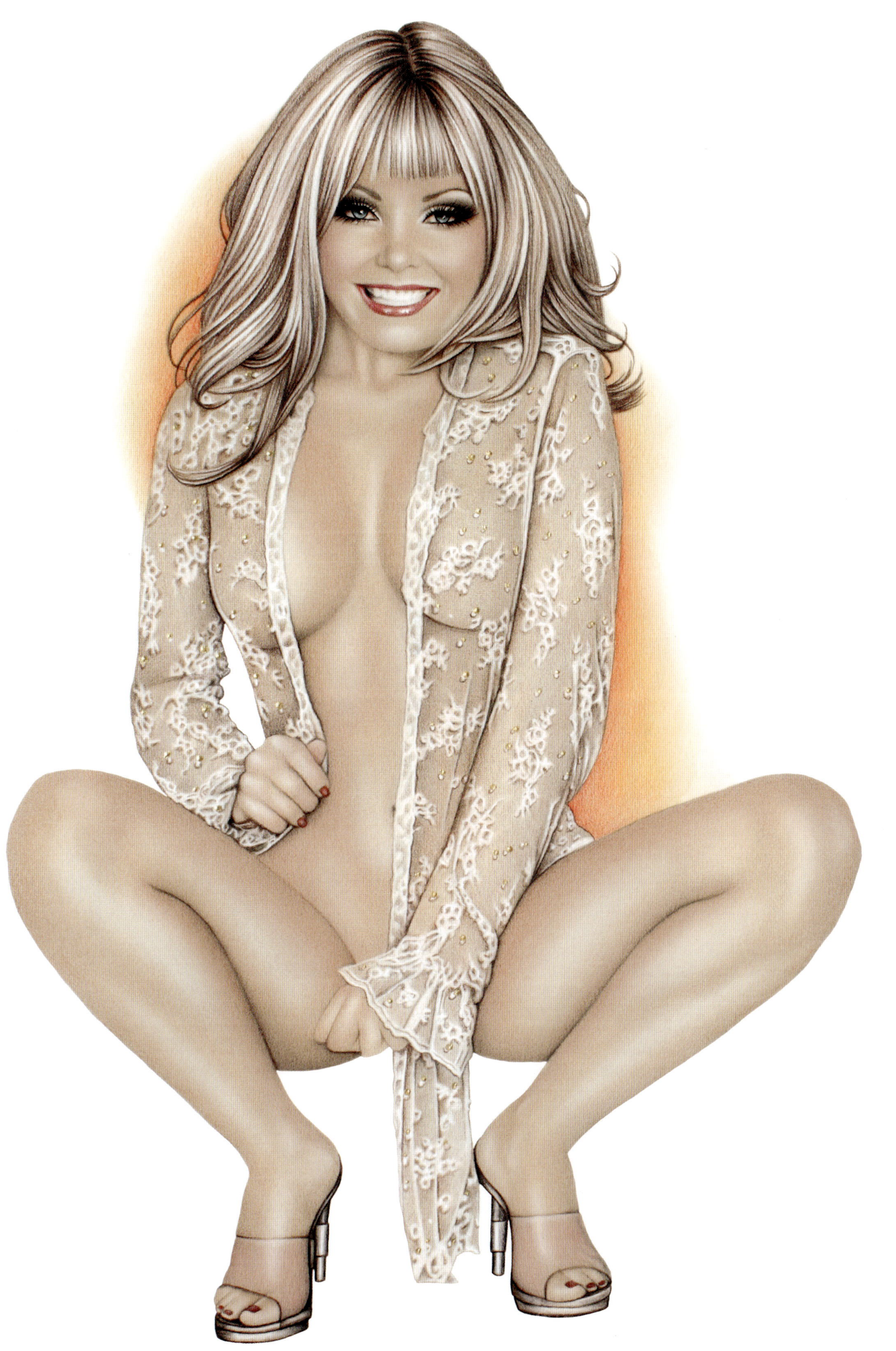

Golden Touch

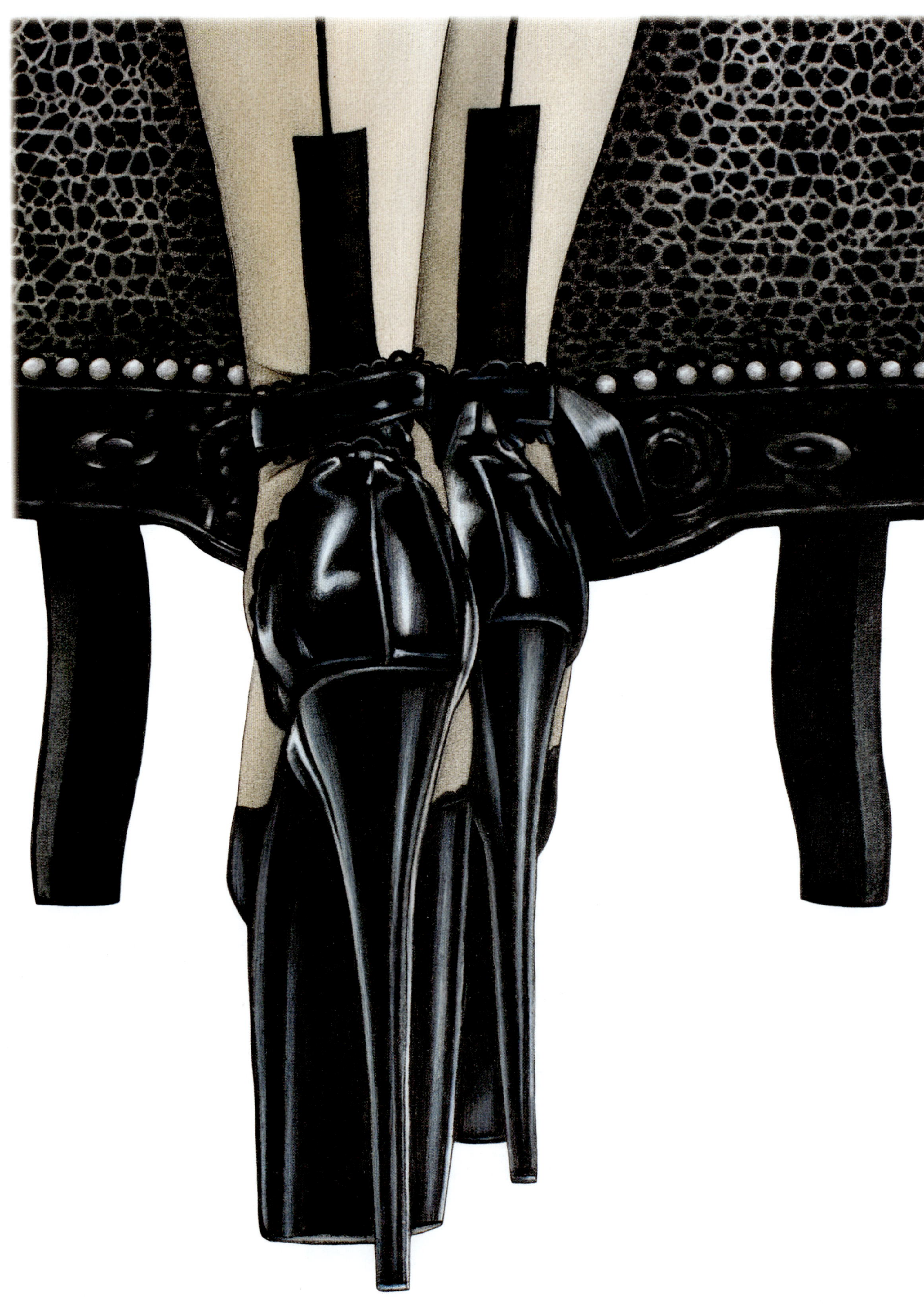

Stiletto

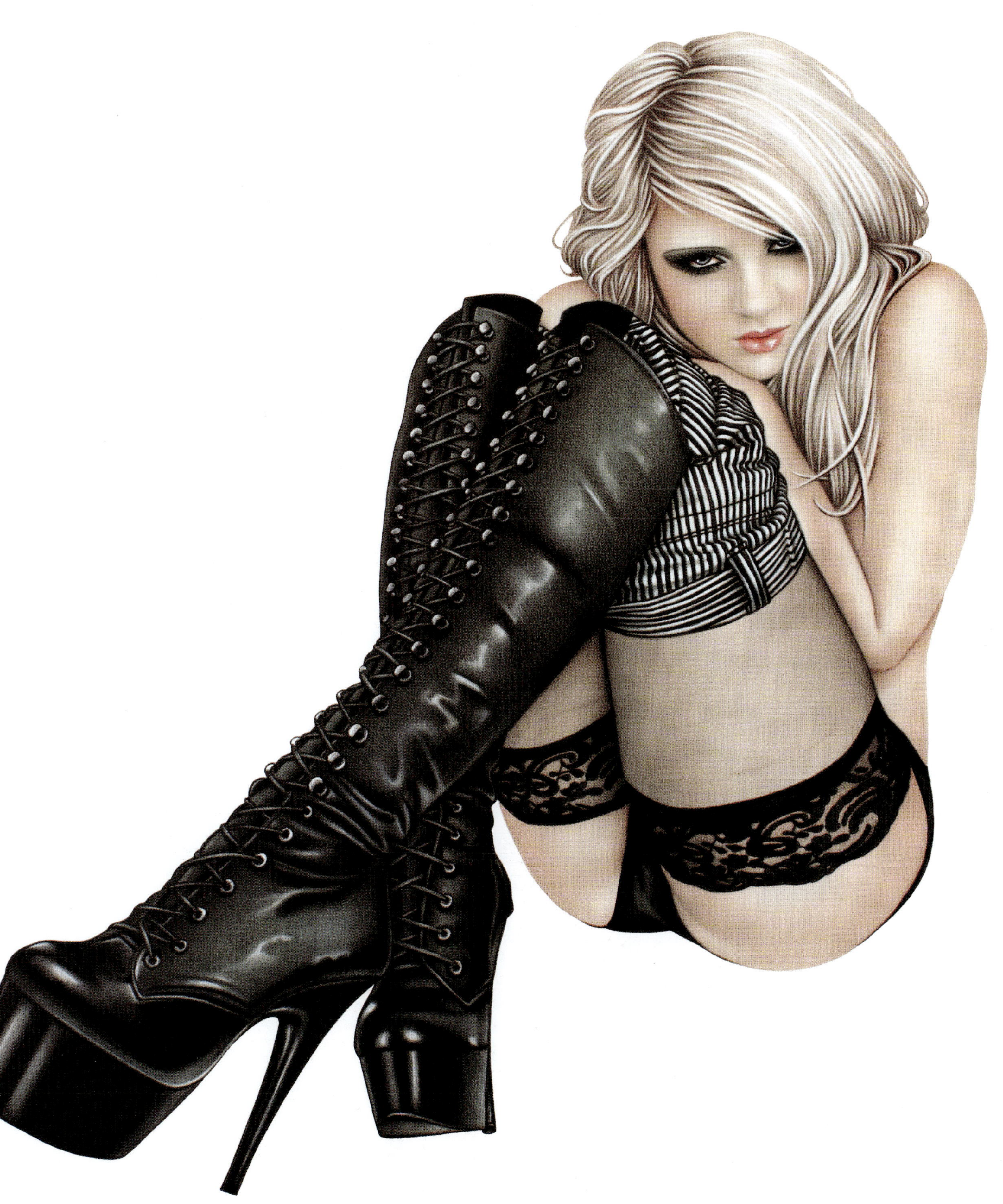

Shrinking Violet

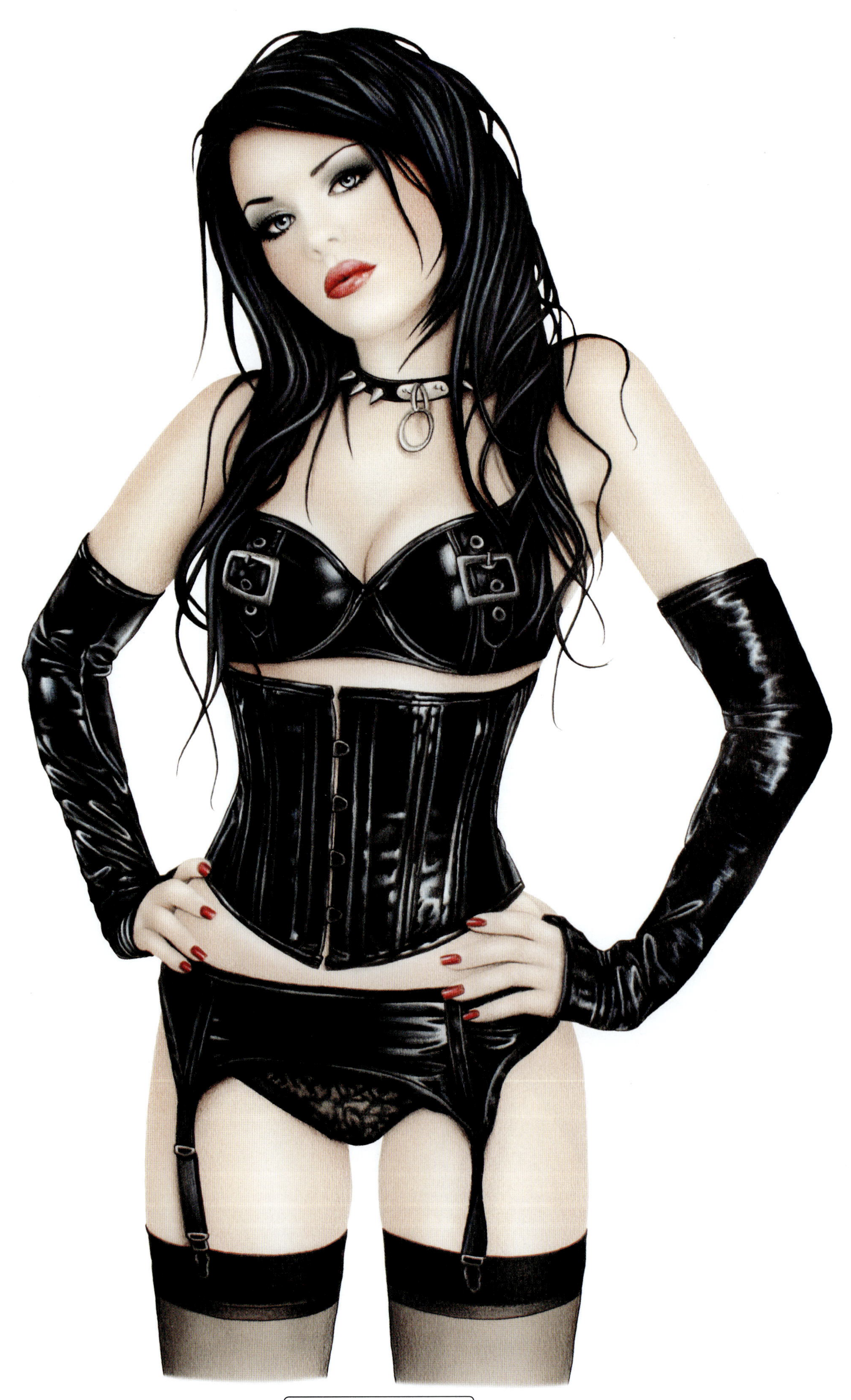

Defiance

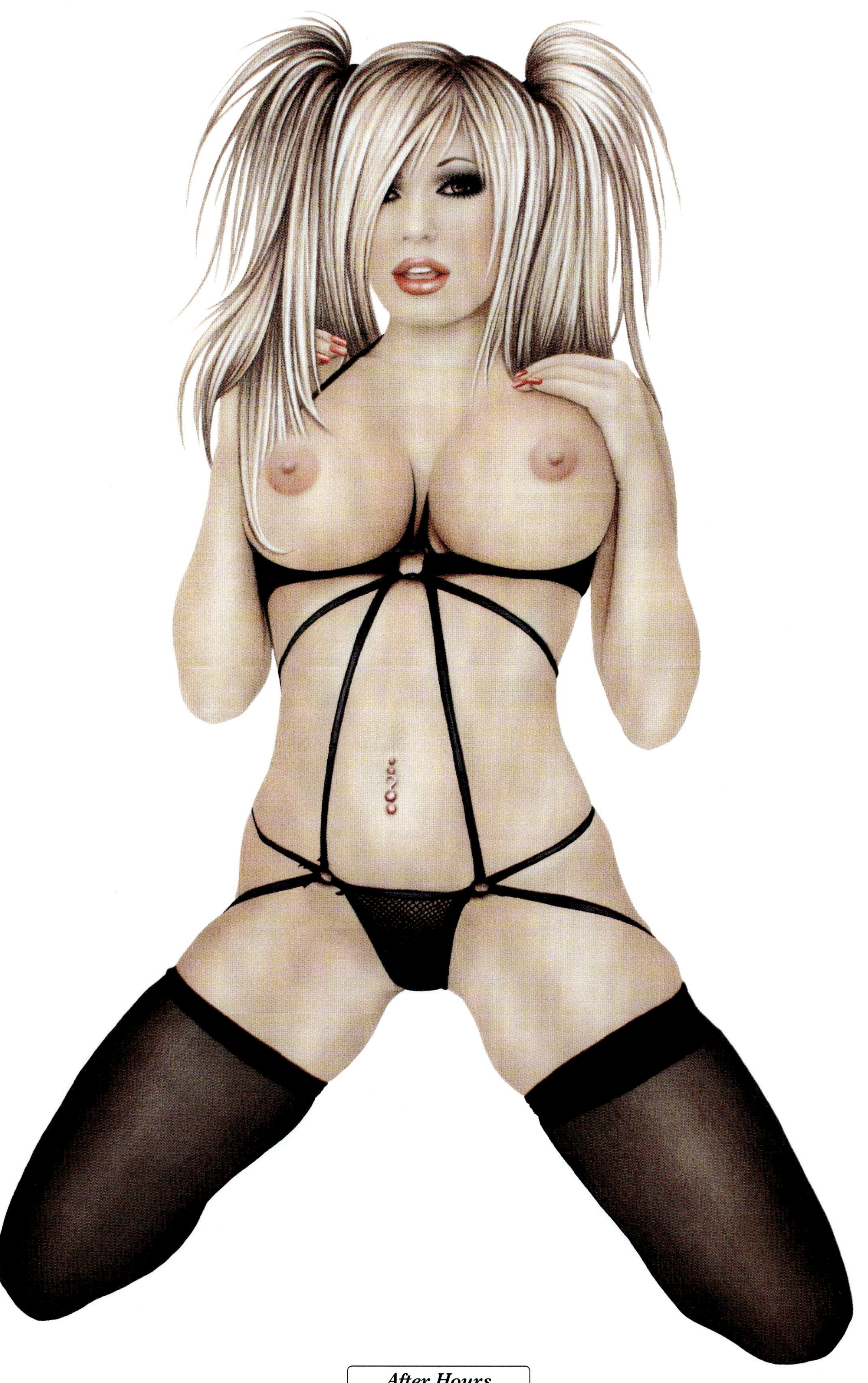

After Hours

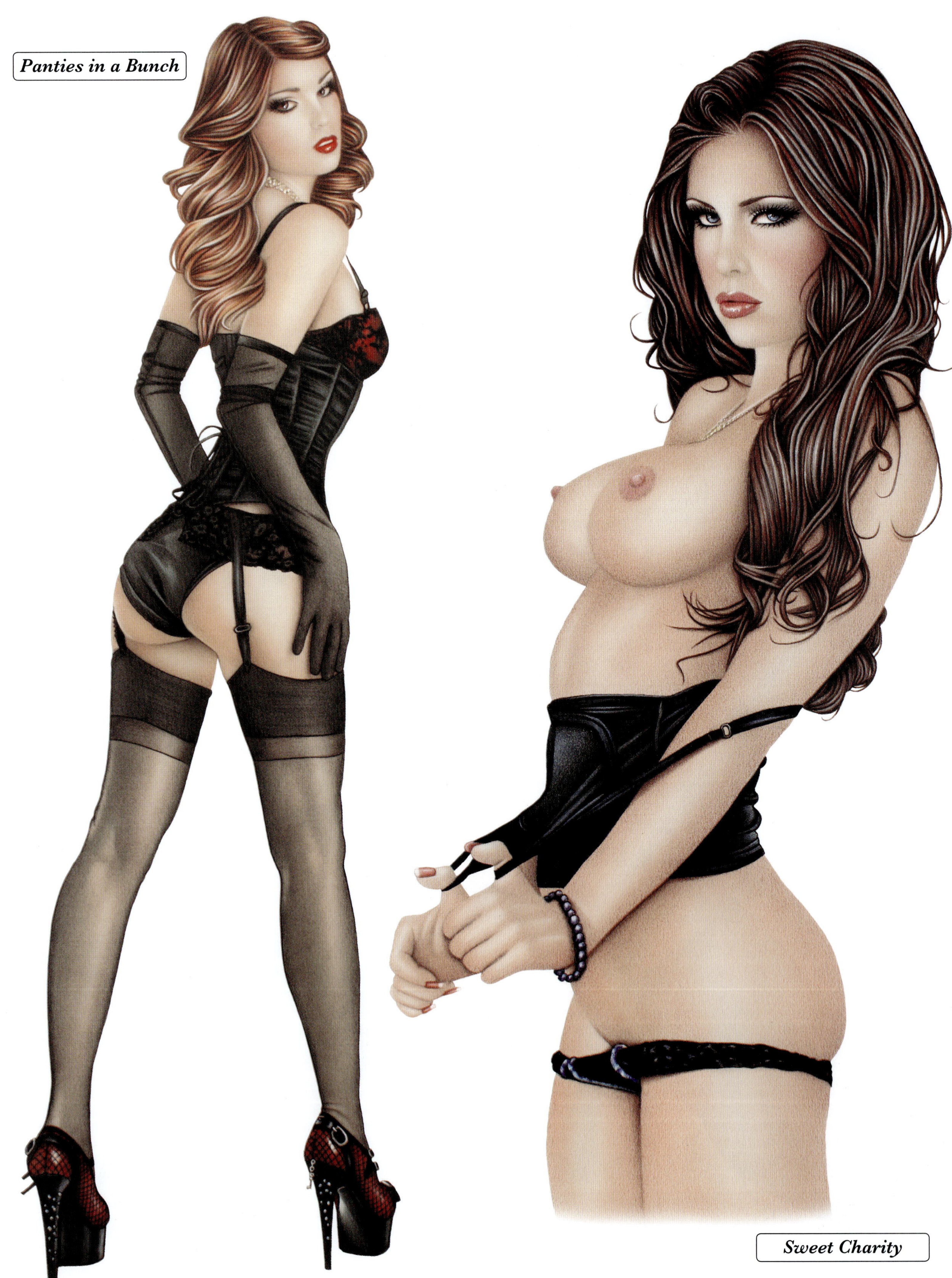
Panties in a Bunch
Sweet Charity

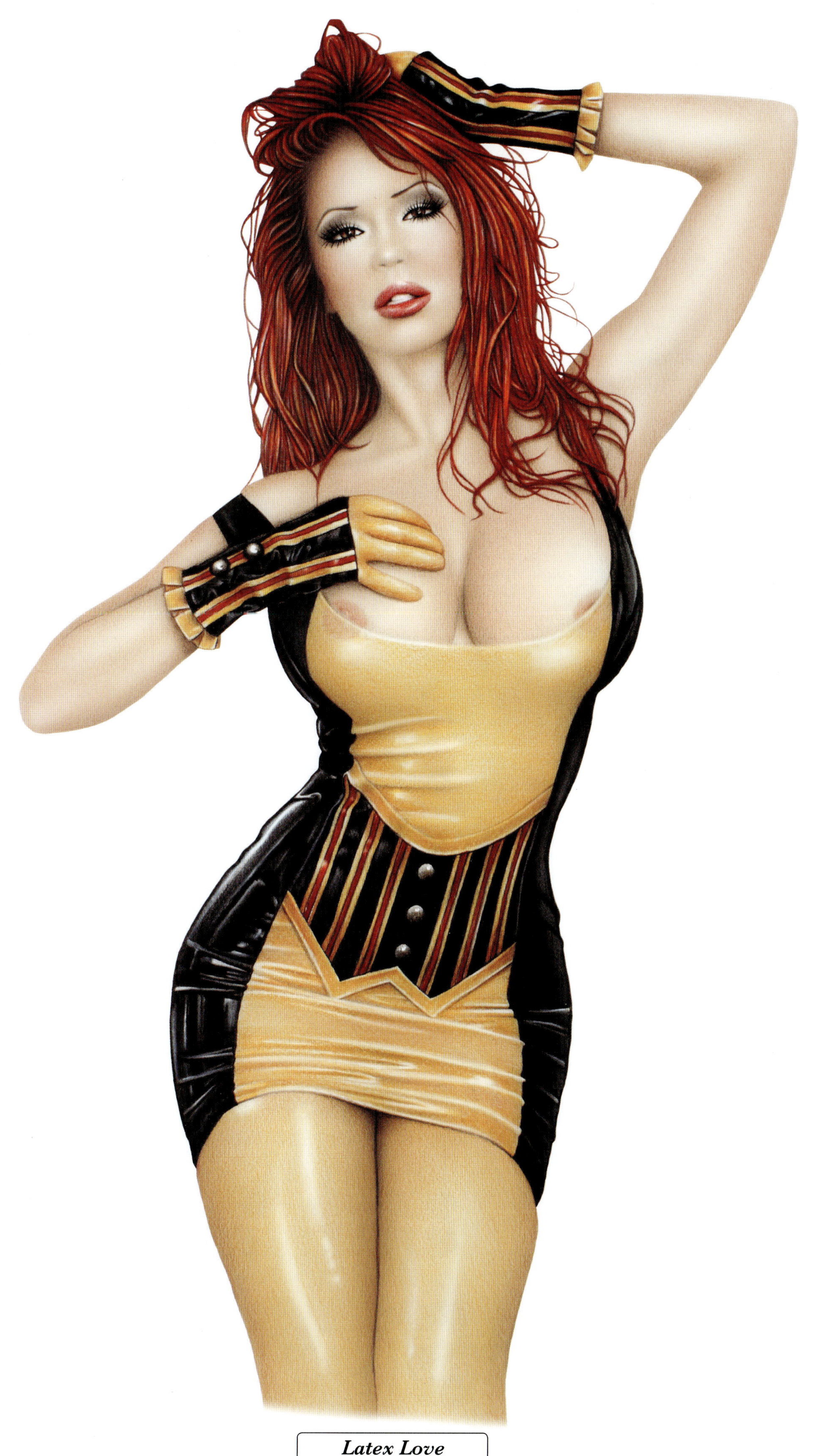

Latex Love

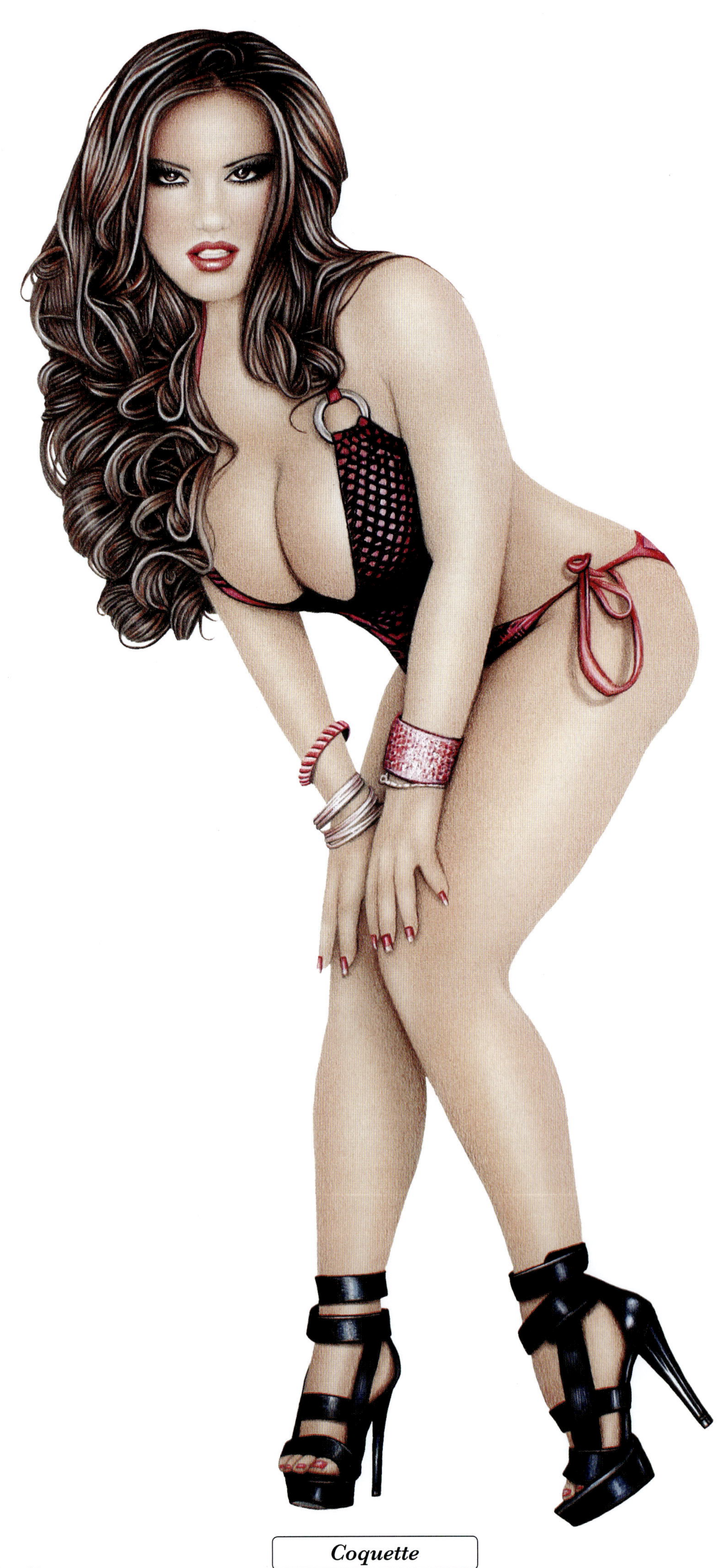

Coquette

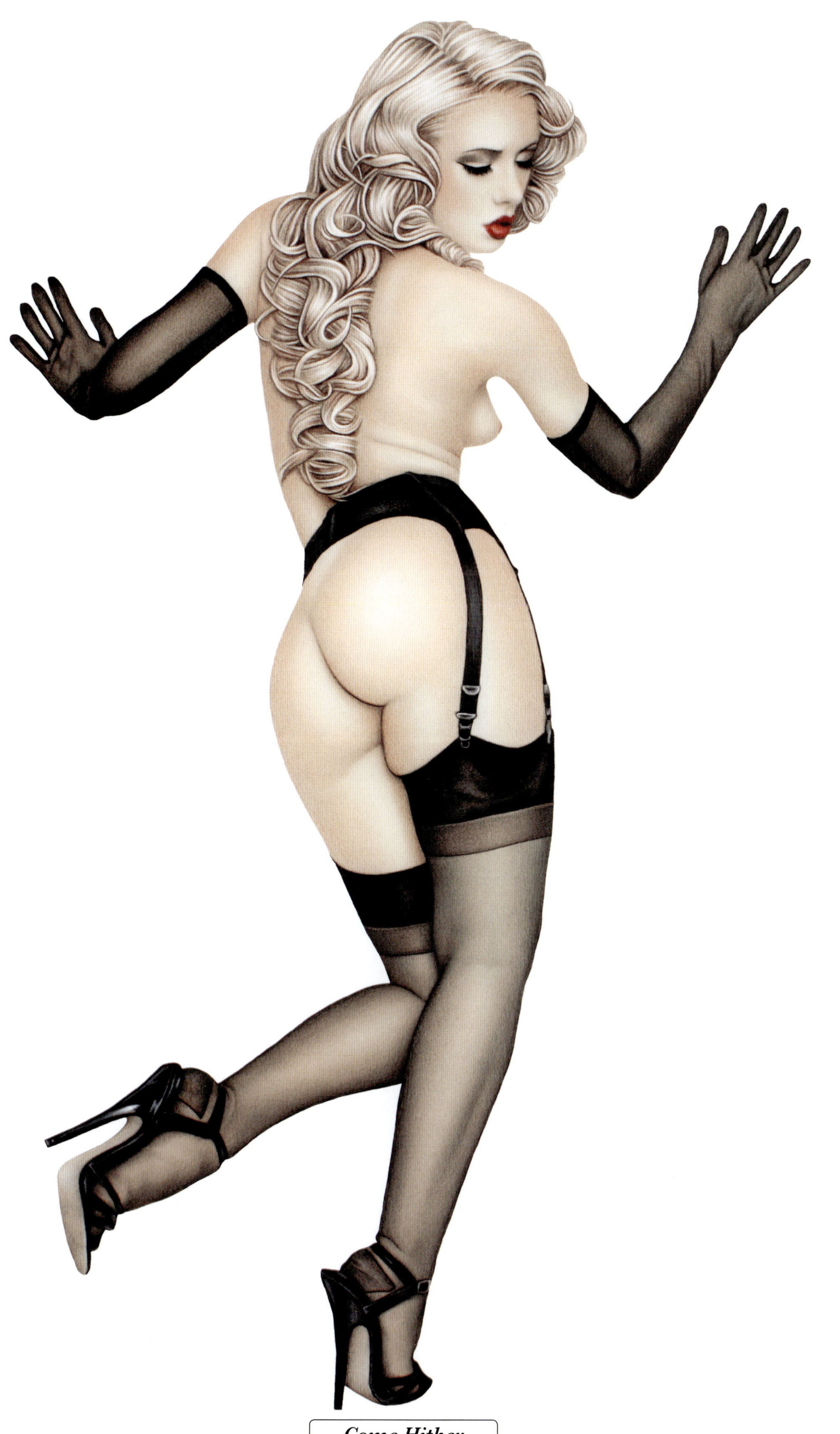

Come Hither

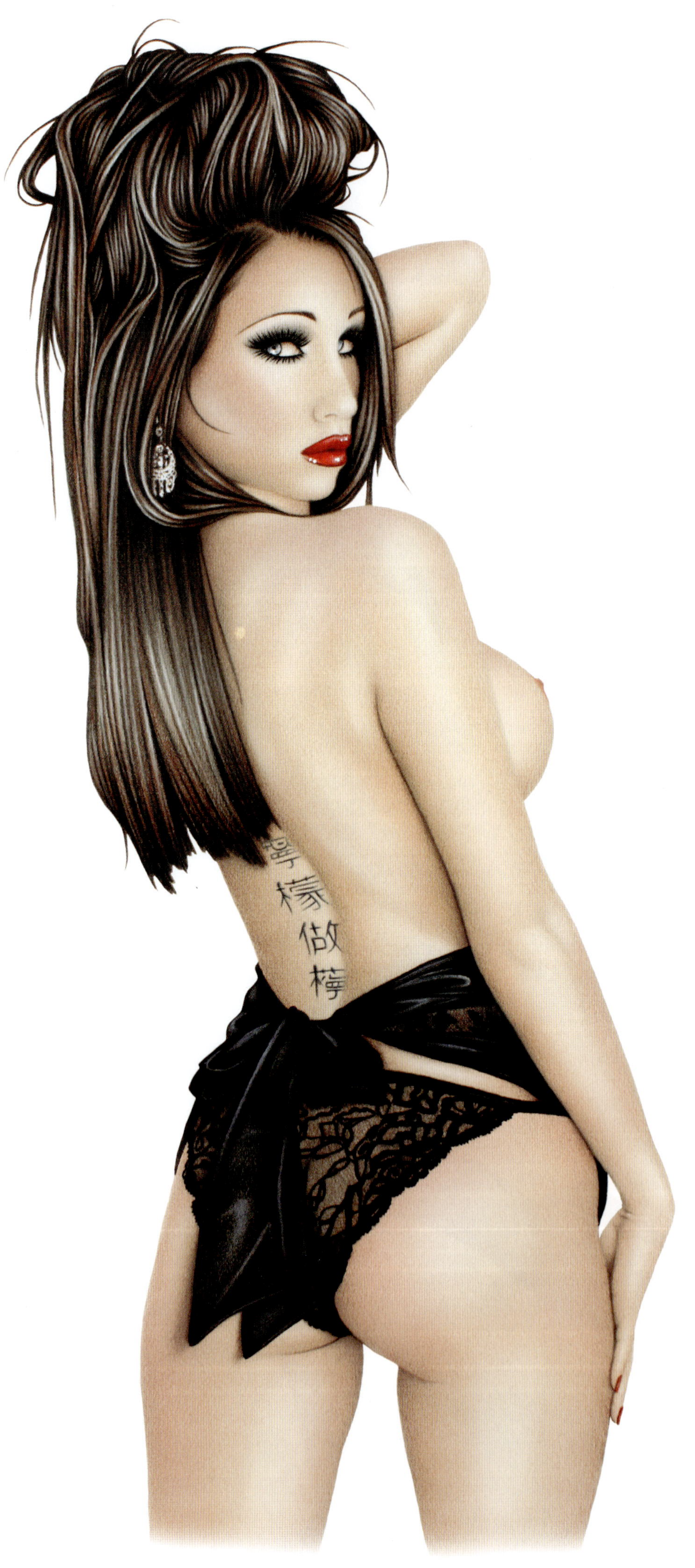

Poof

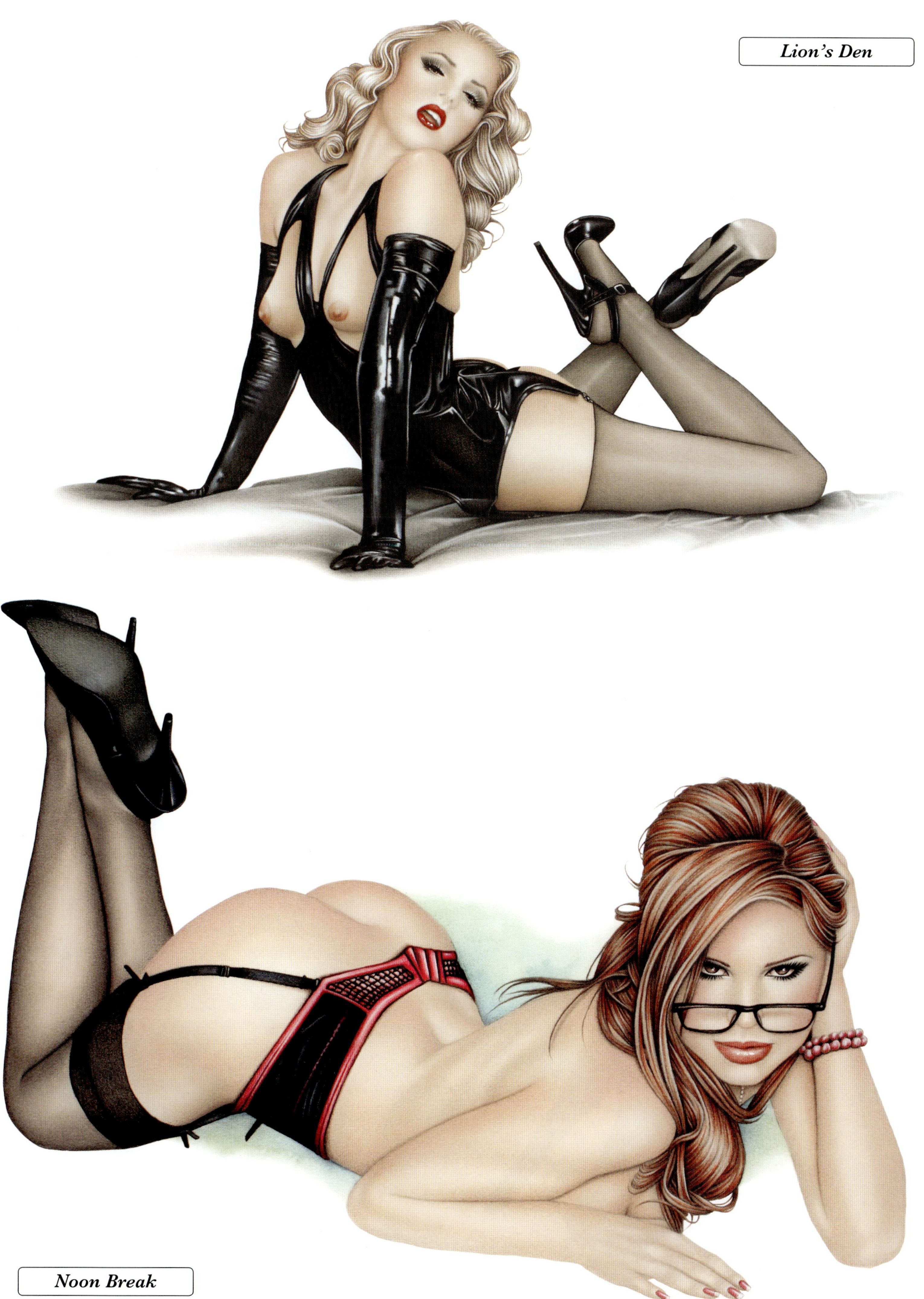

Lion's Den

Noon Break

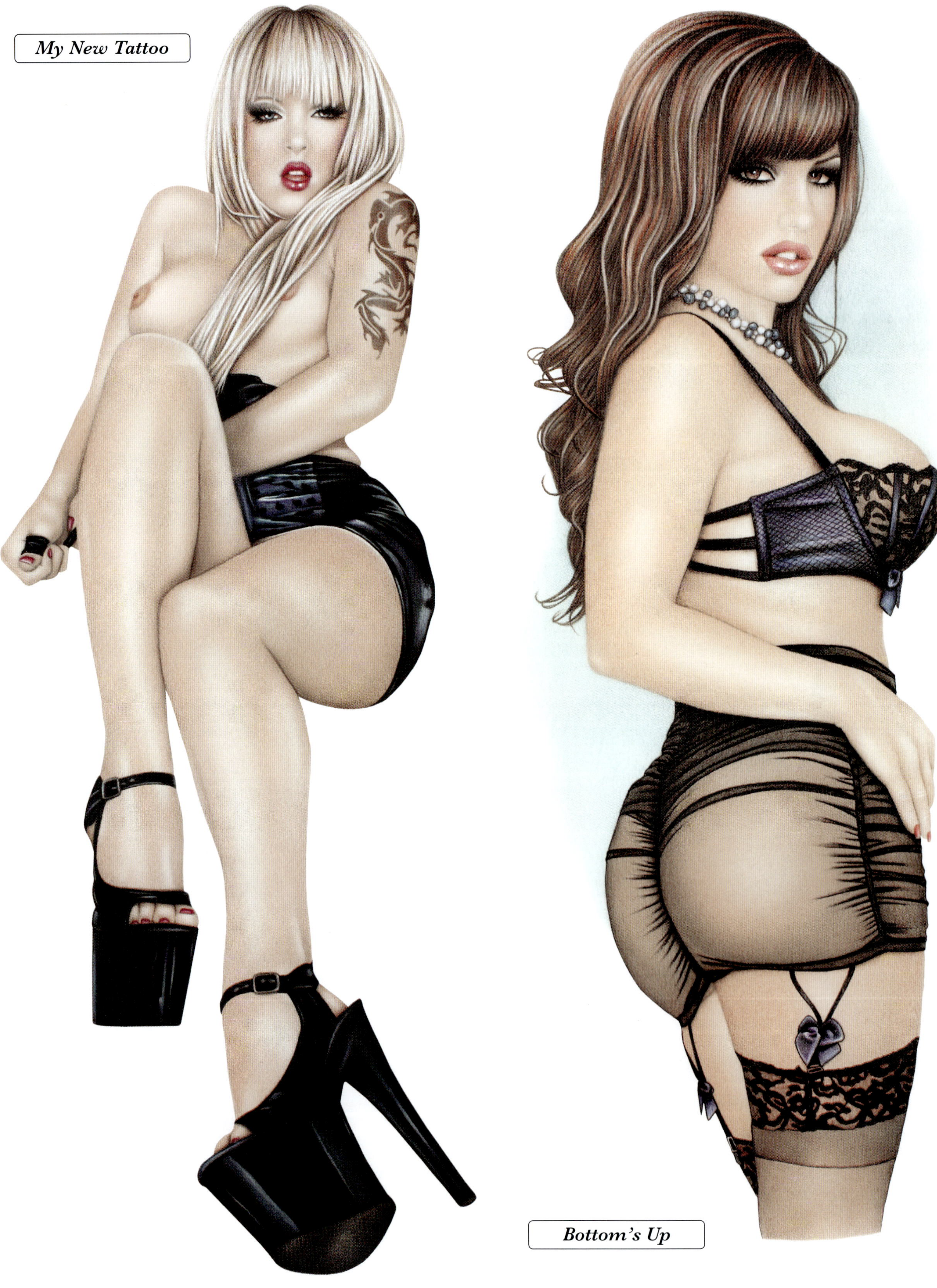

My New Tattoo

Bottom's Up

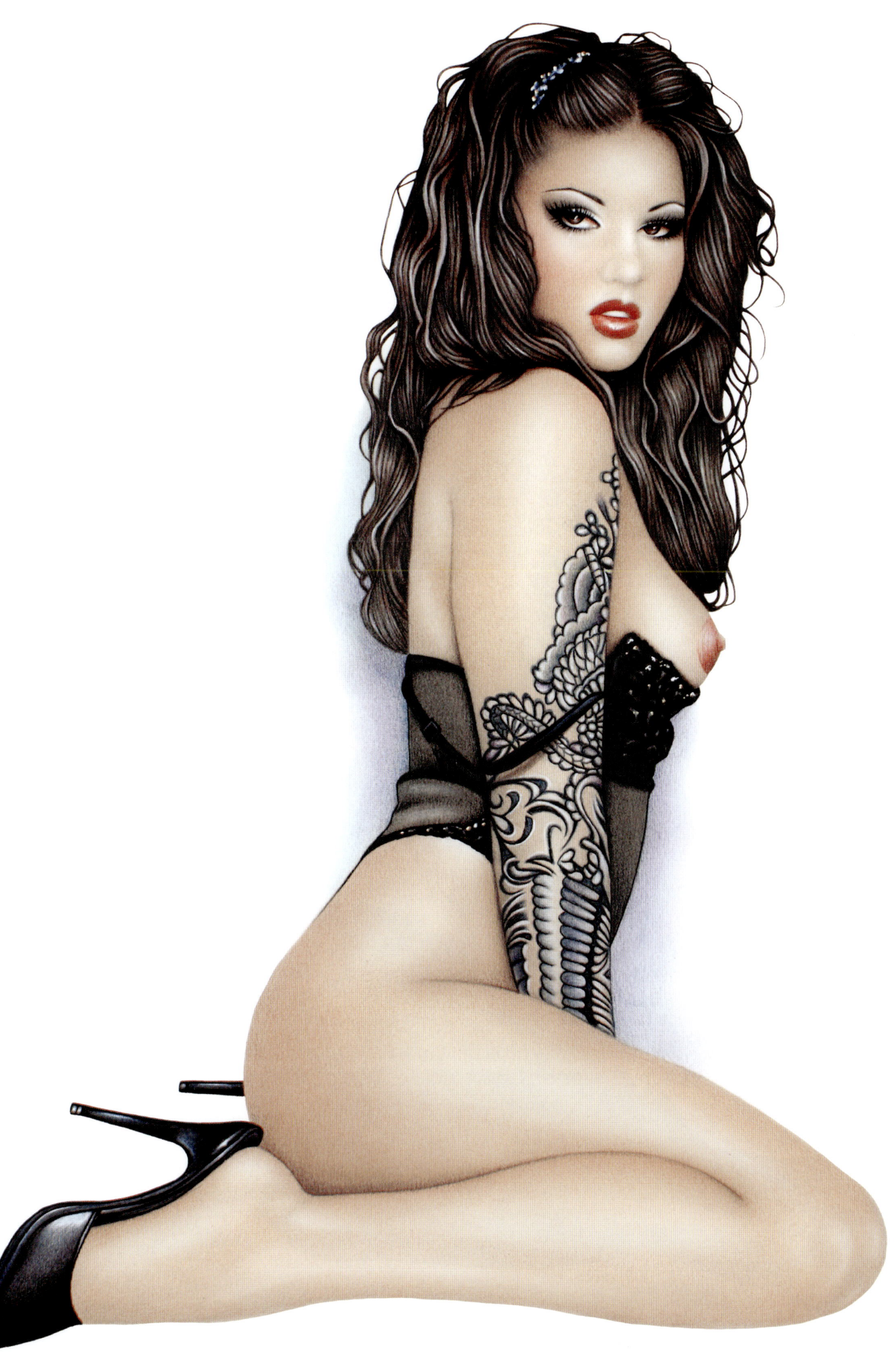

Inkling

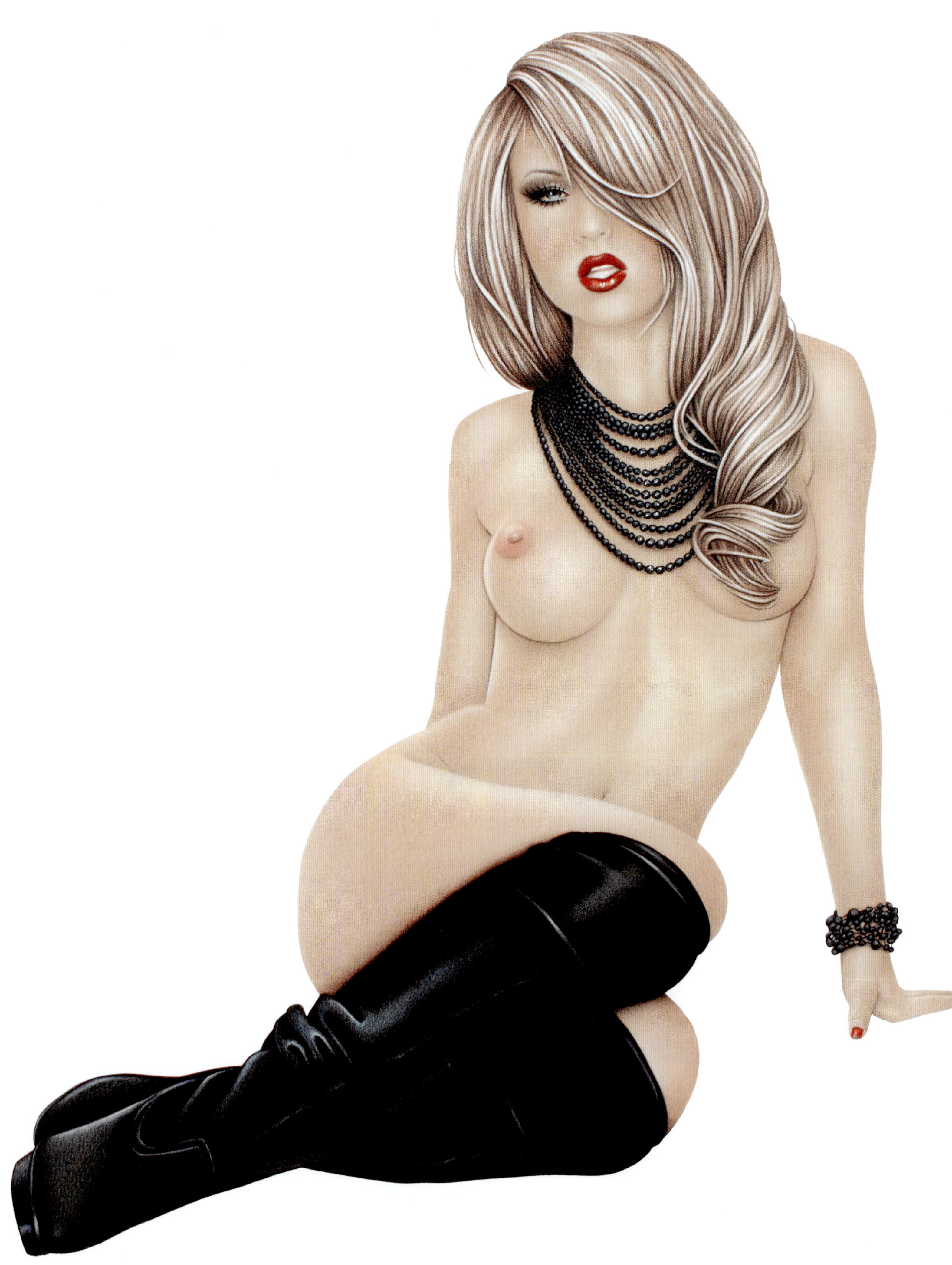

Black Pearl

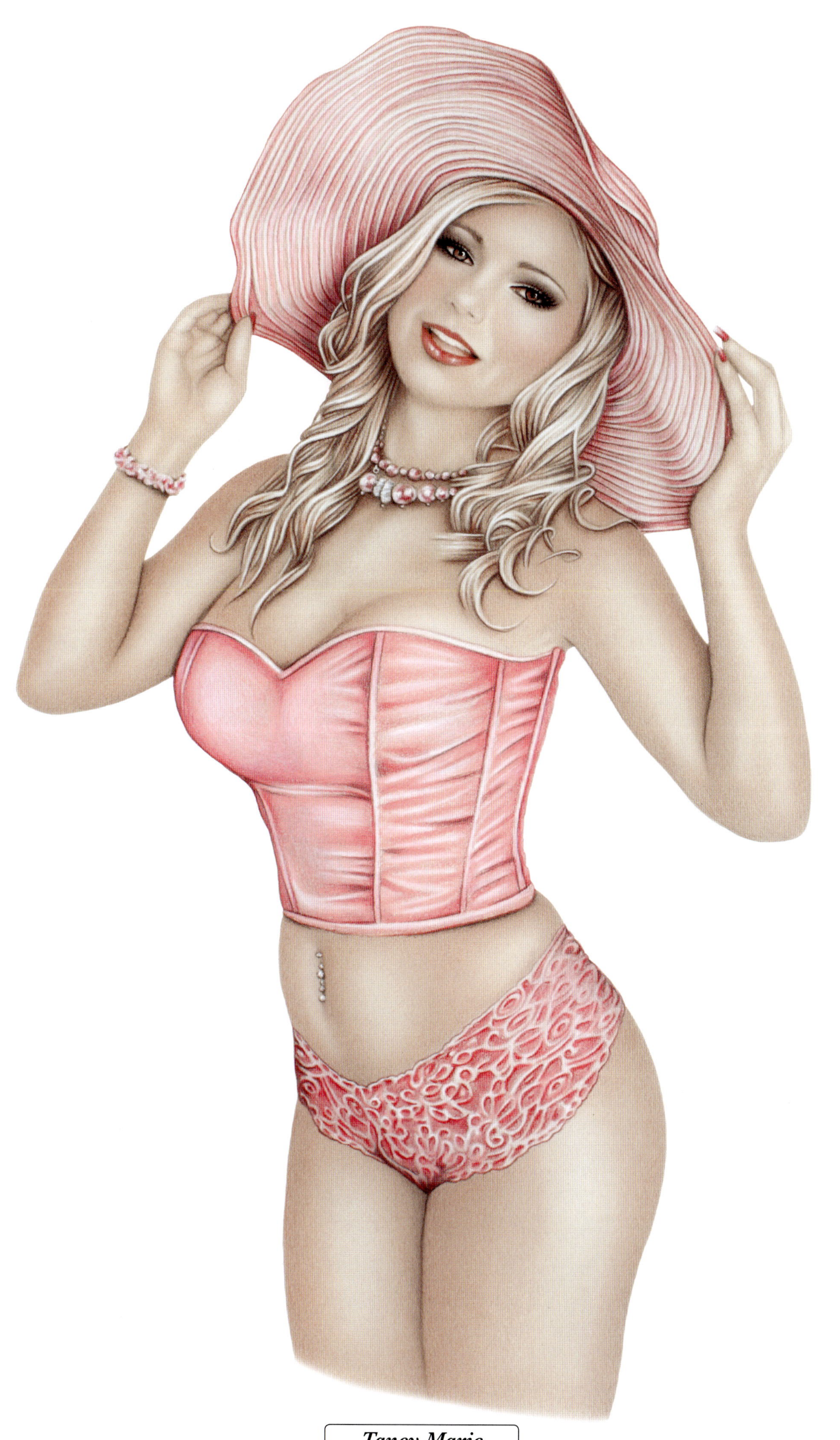

Tancy Marie

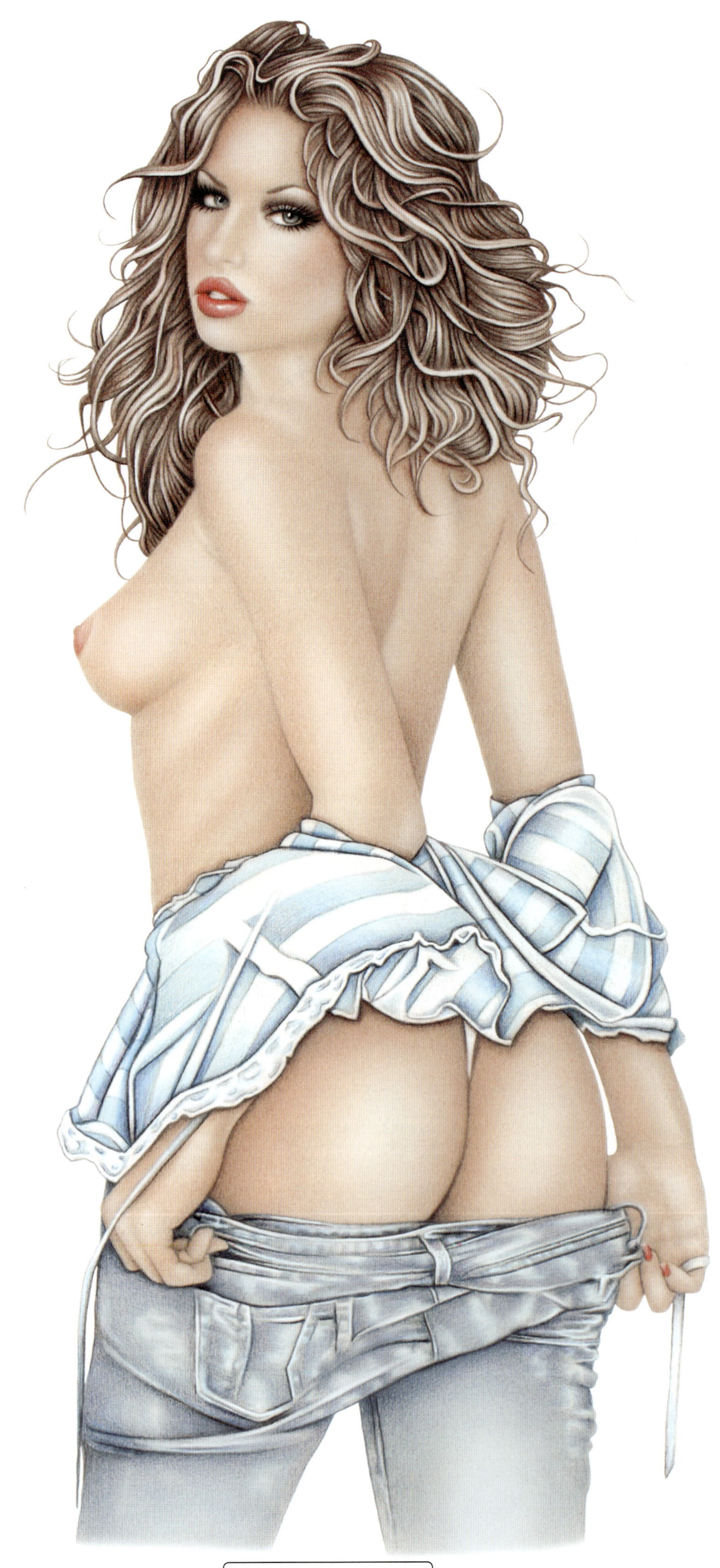

Blueberry Pie

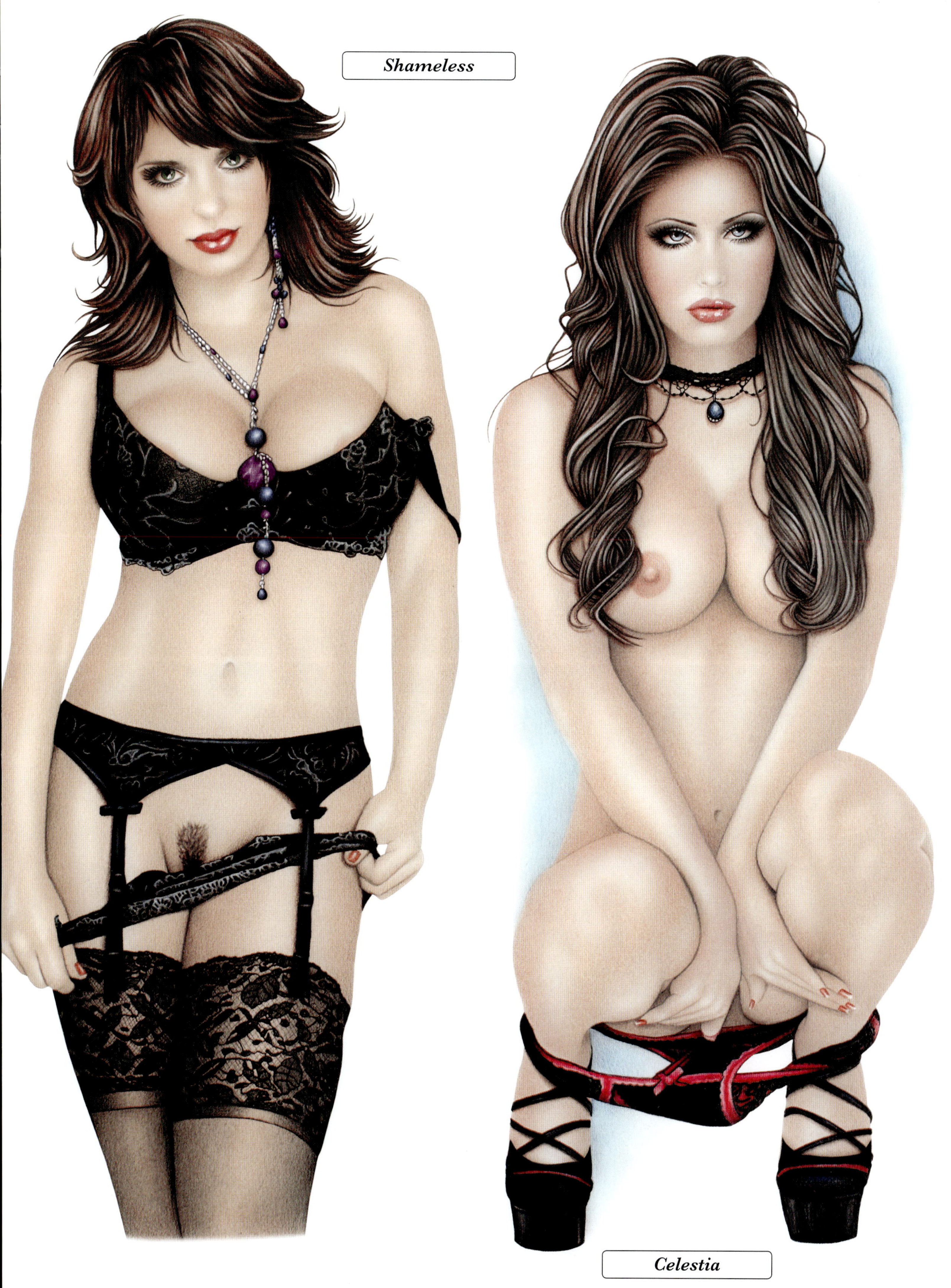

Shameless

Celestia

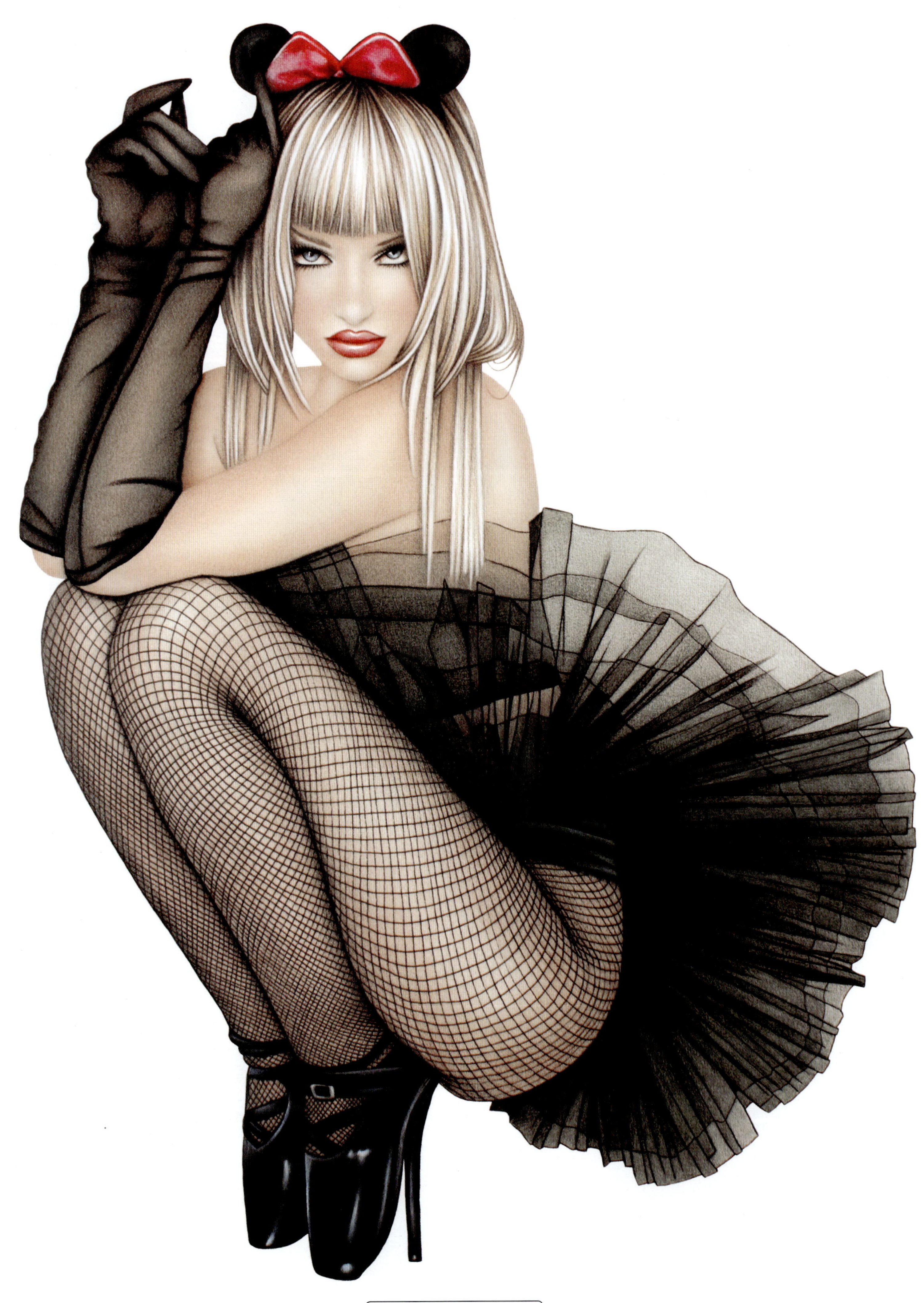

Little Ballerina

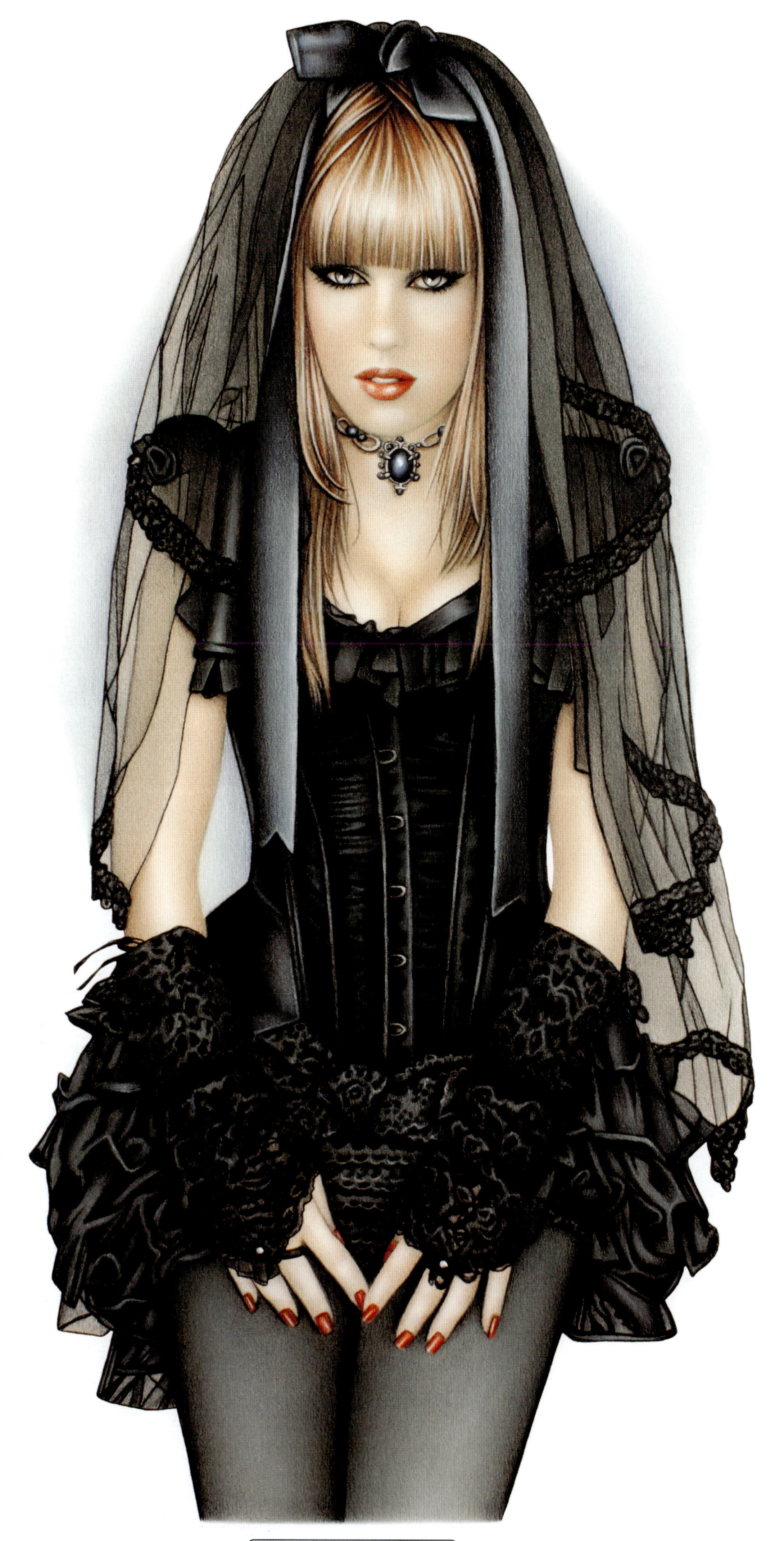

Midnight Wedding

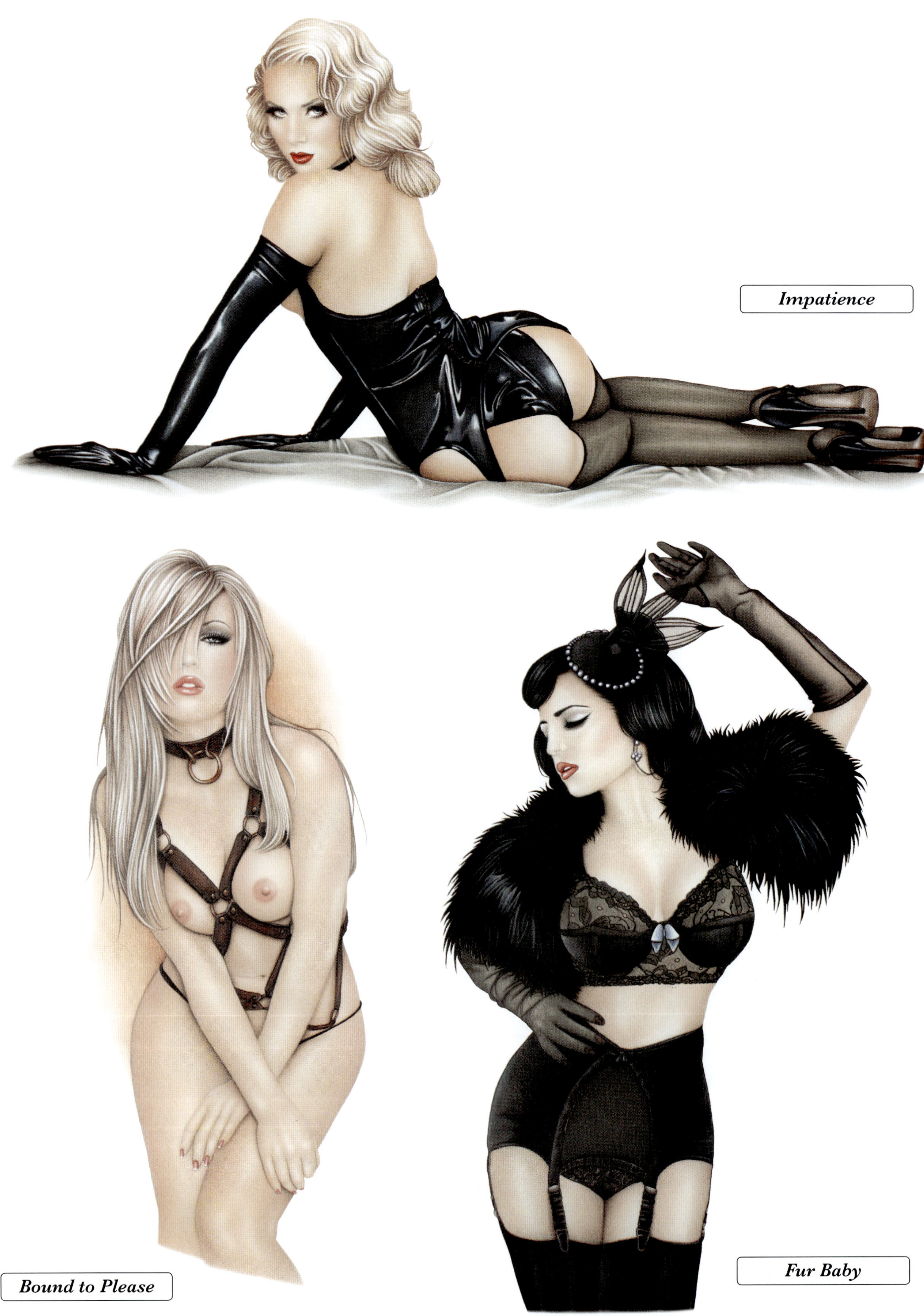
Impatience
Bound to Please
Fur Baby

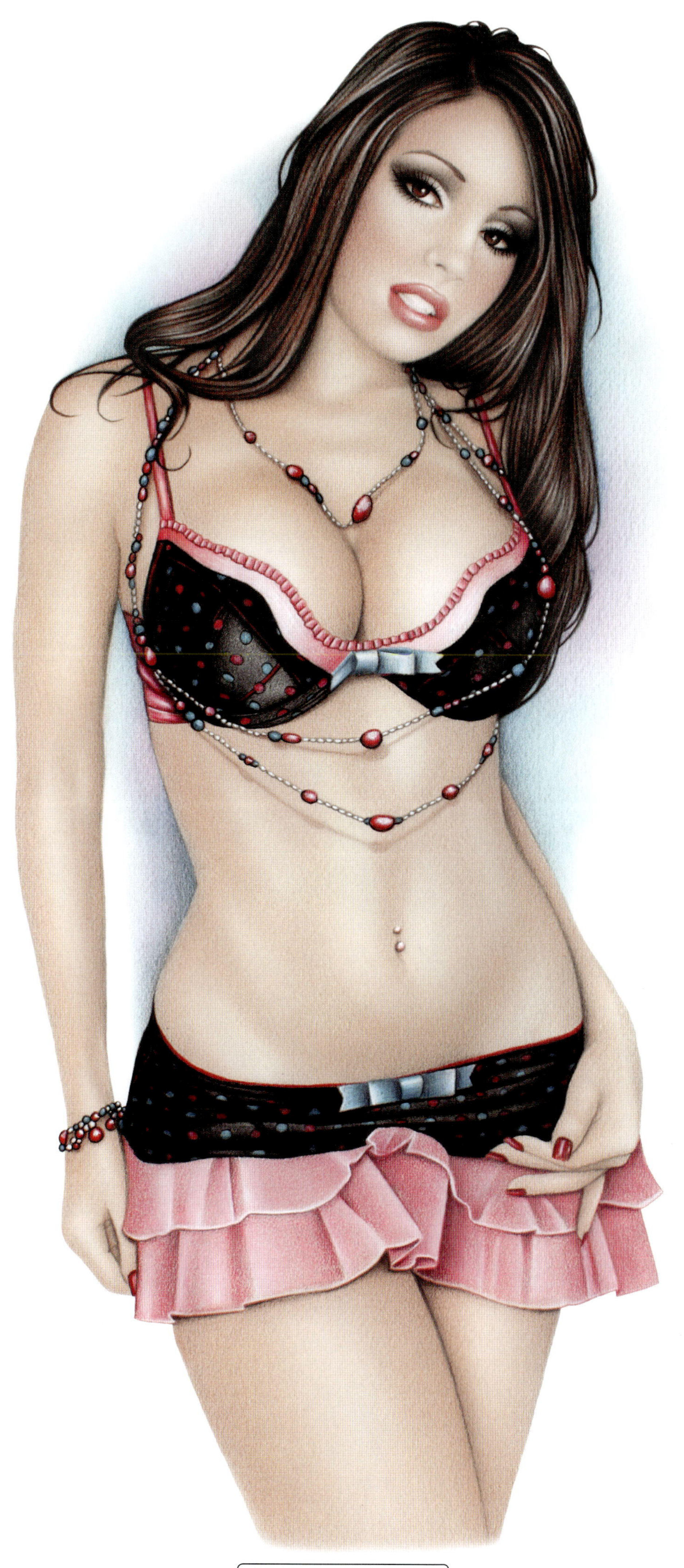

Saccharine

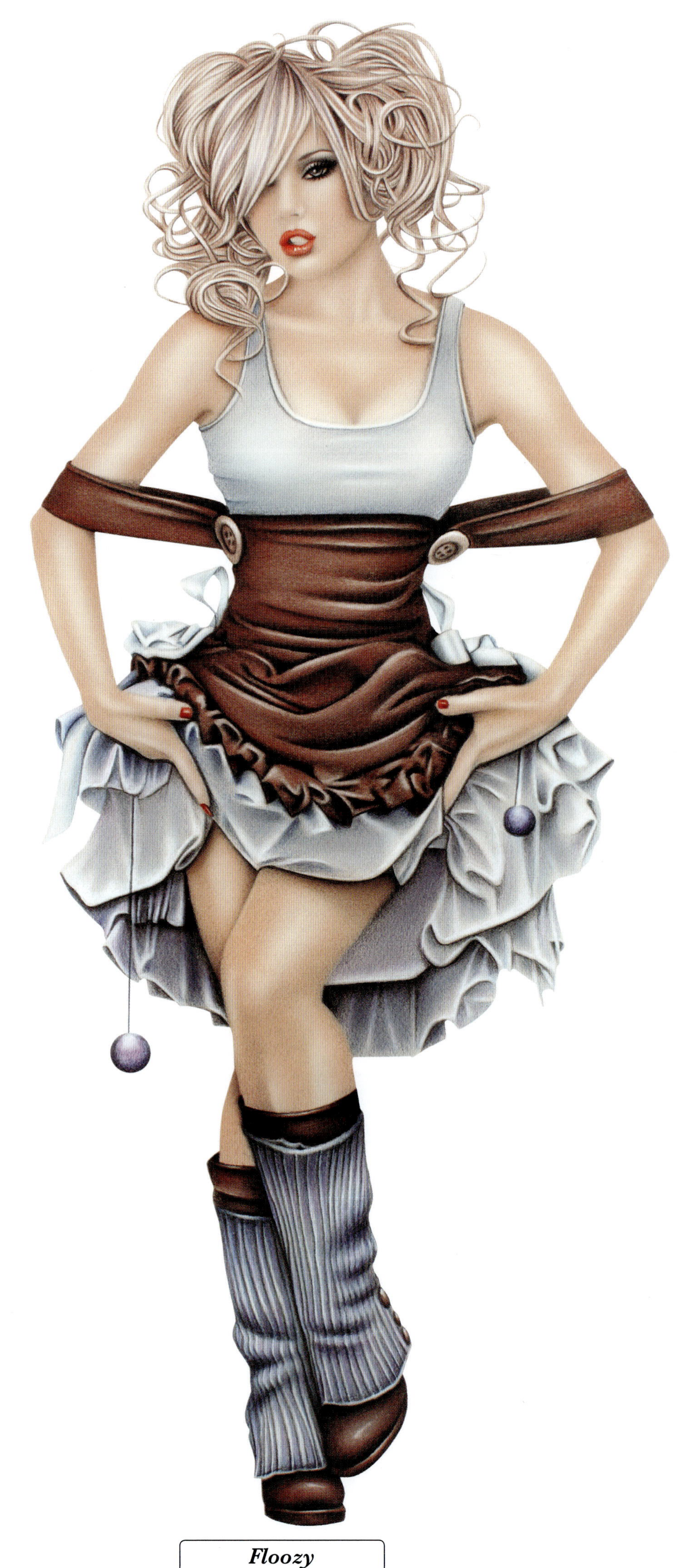

Floozy

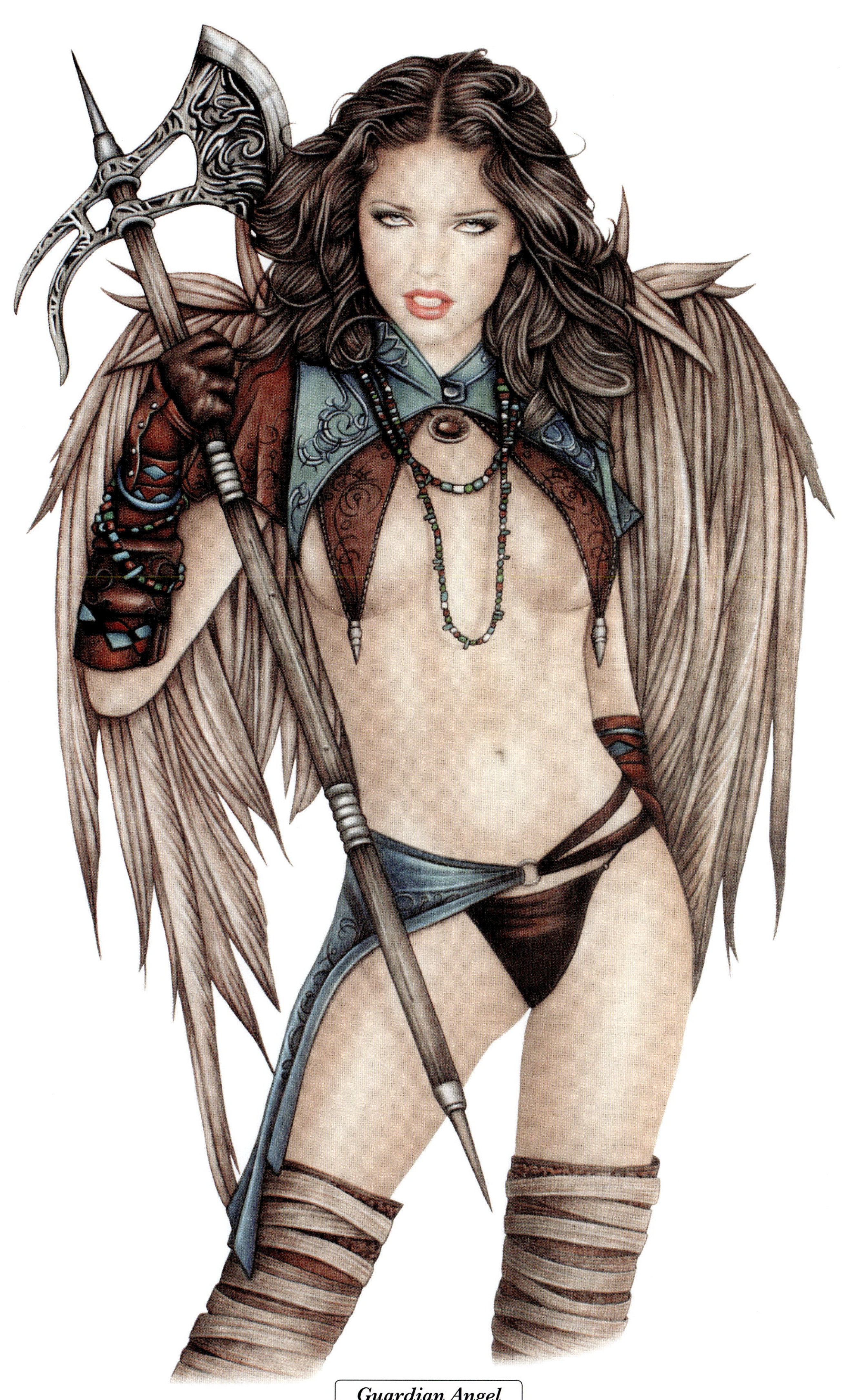

Guardian Angel

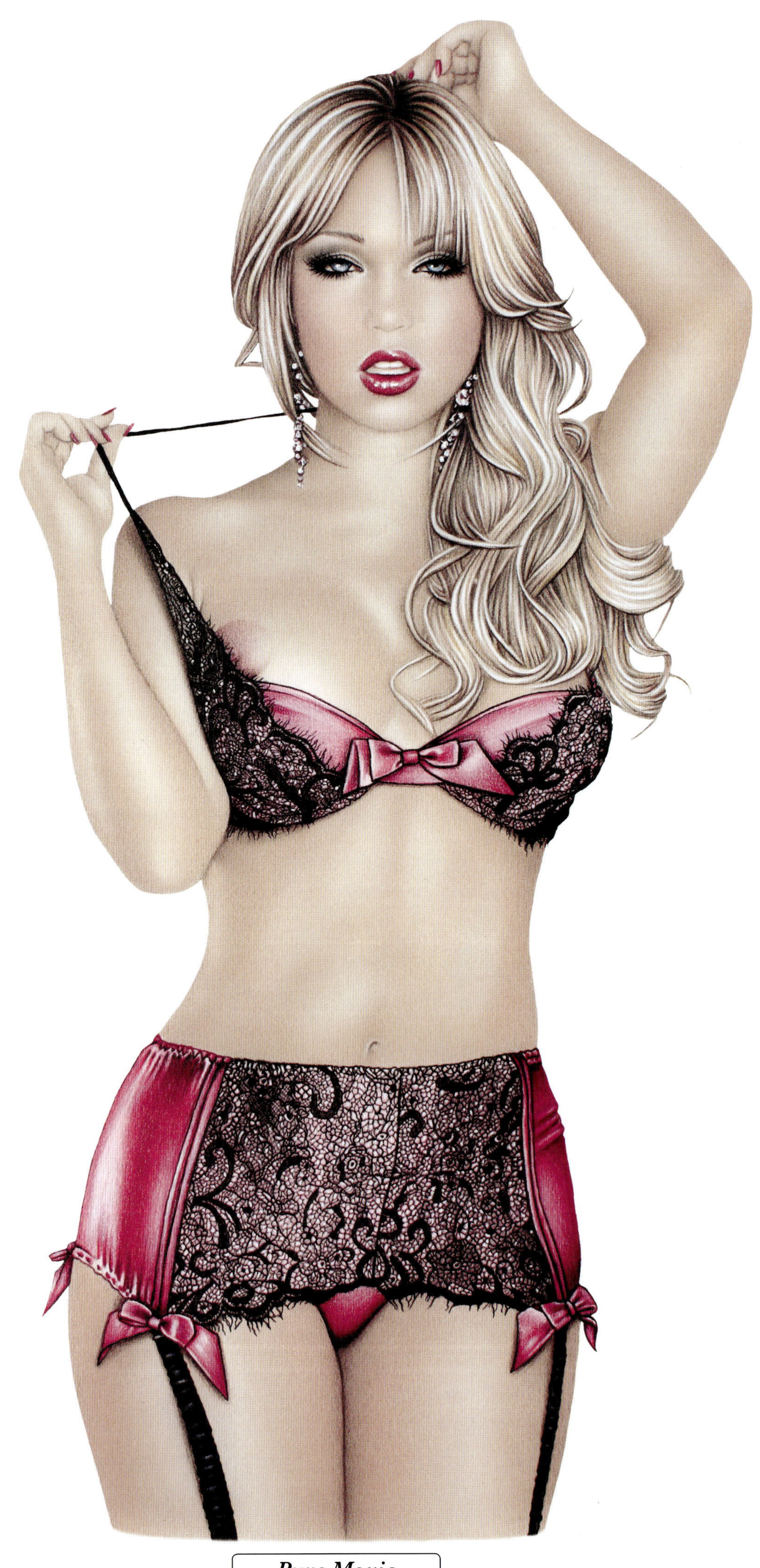

Pure Moxie

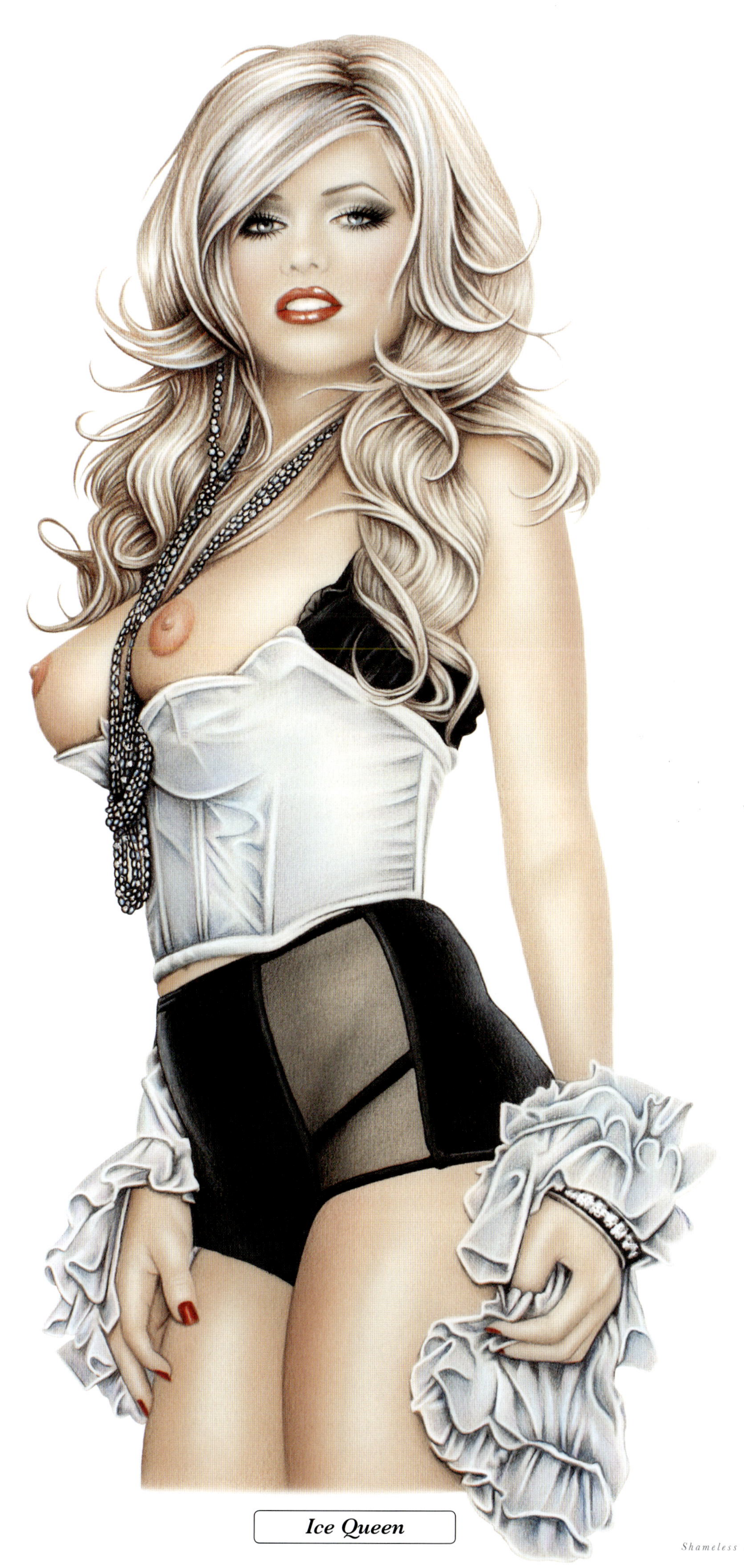

Ice Queen

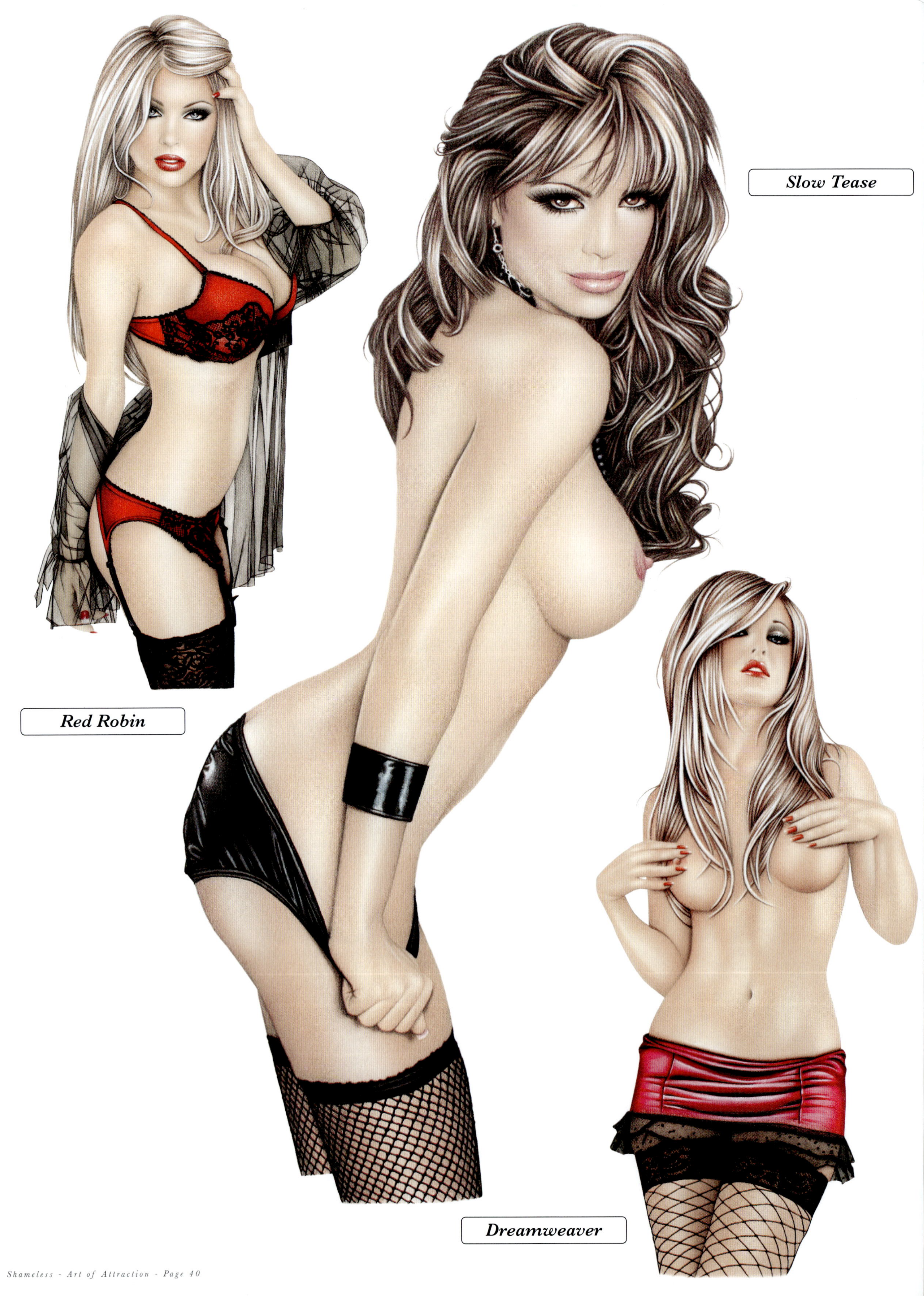
Slow Tease
Red Robin
Dreamweaver

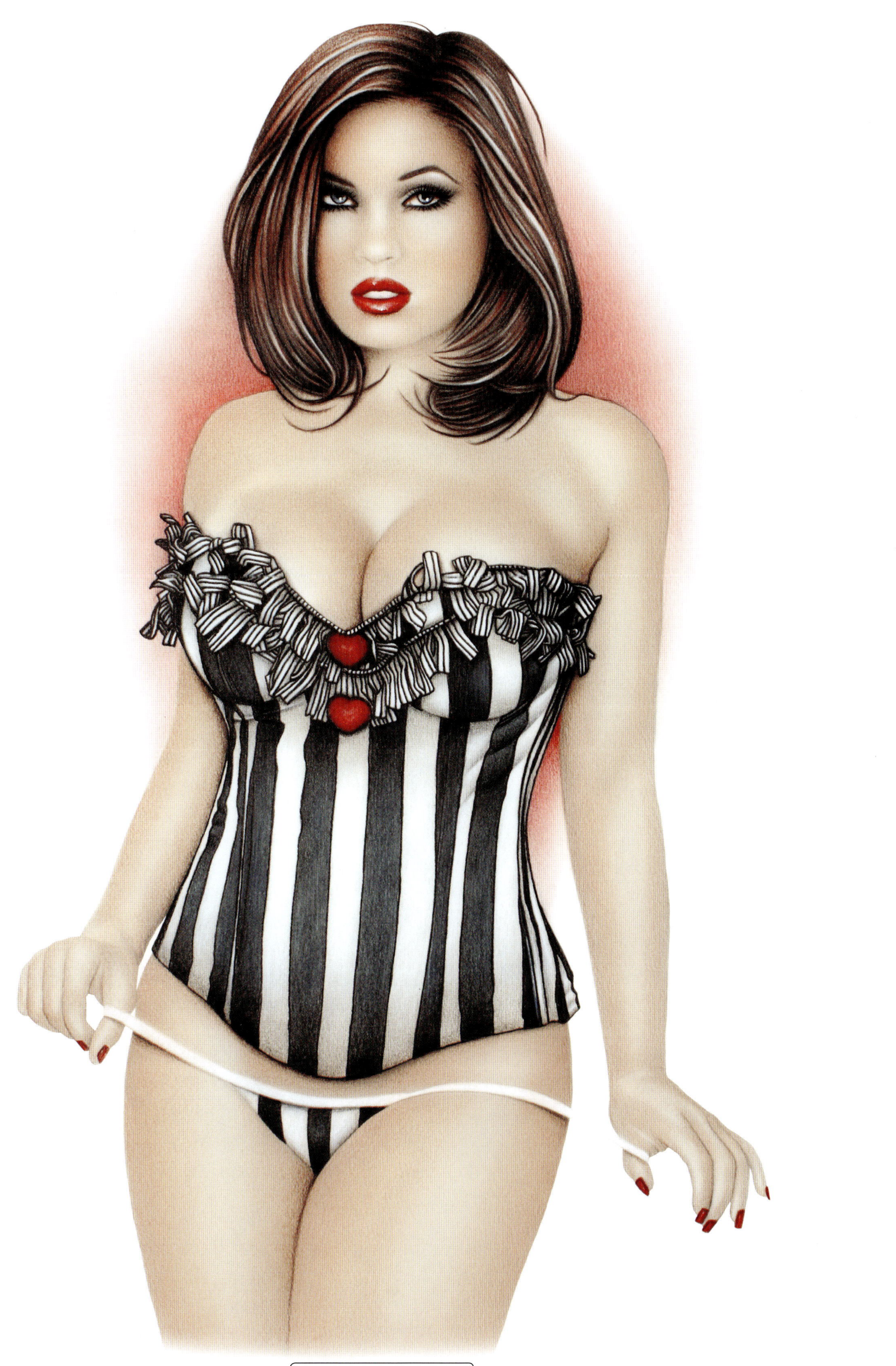

Cherry Blossom

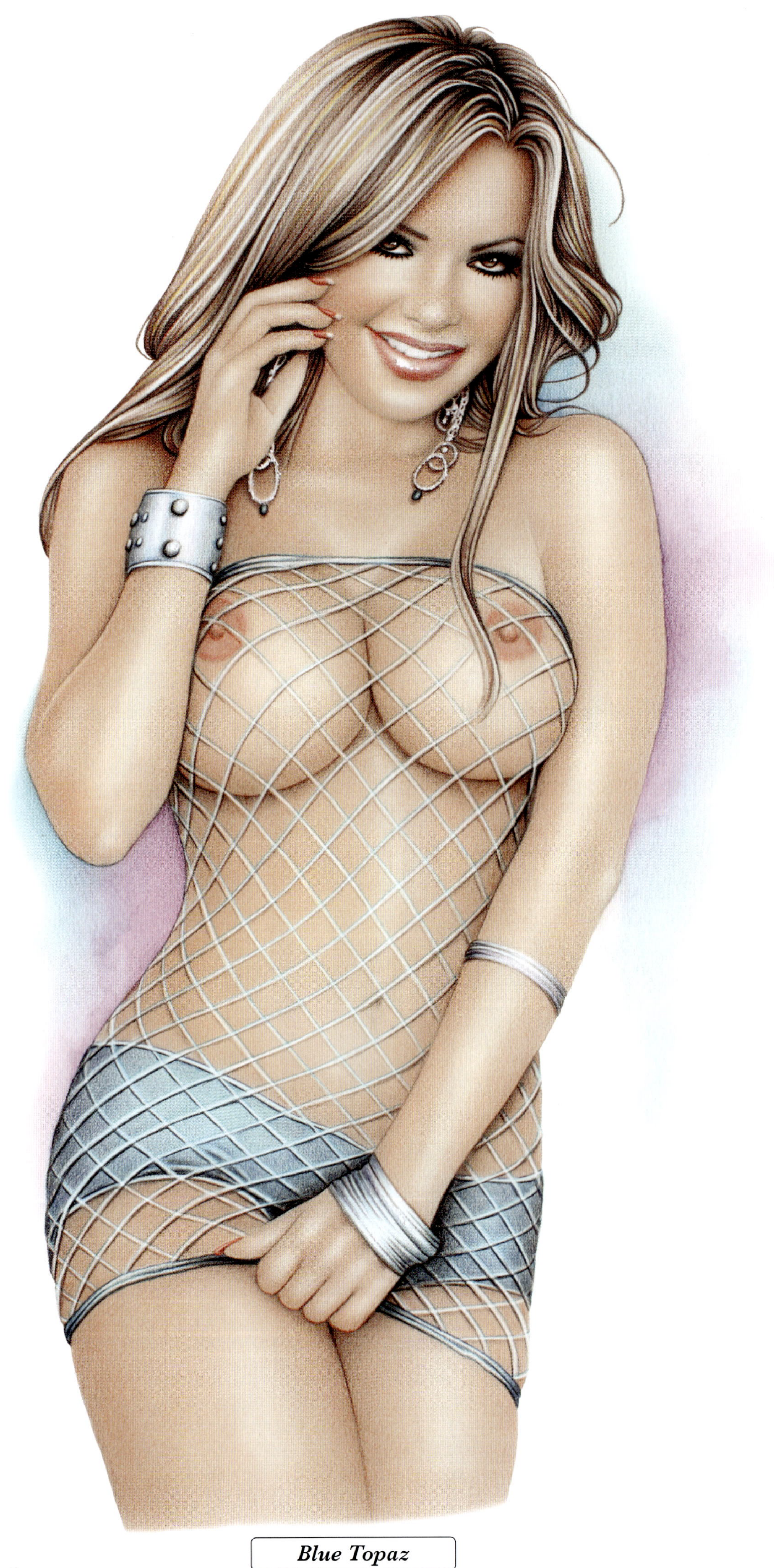

Blue Topaz

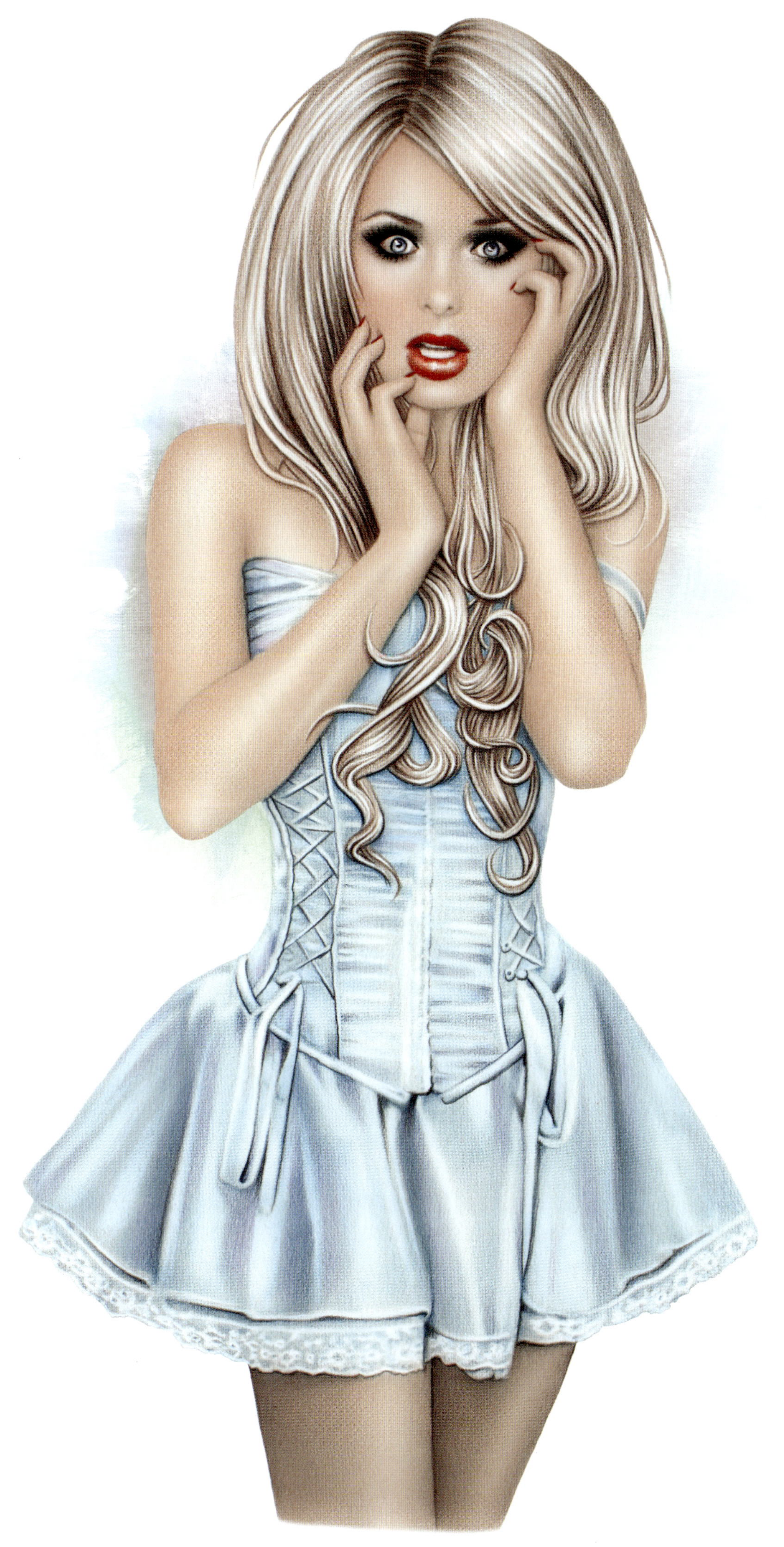

Valerie Virgin

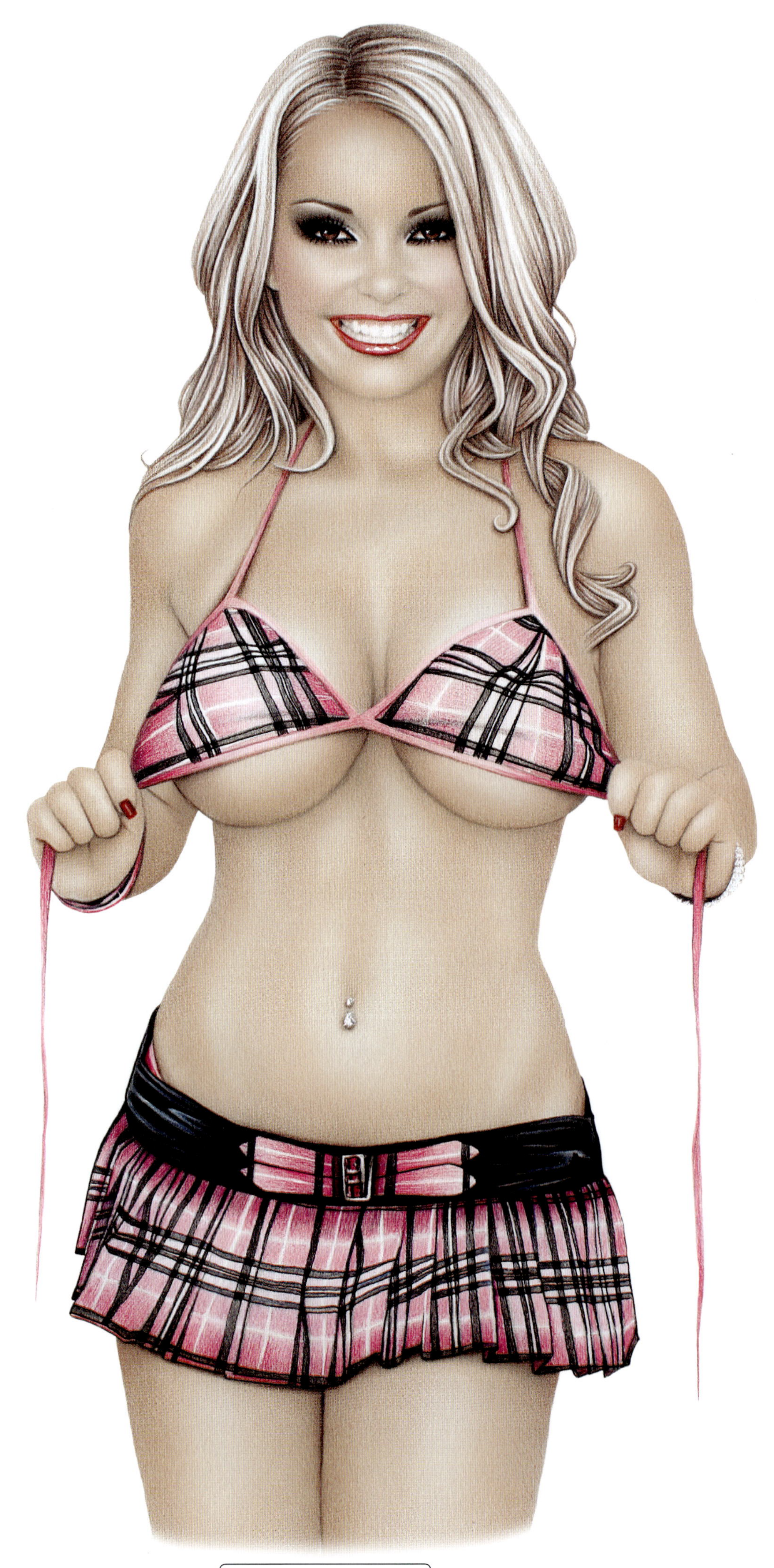

Miss Mischief

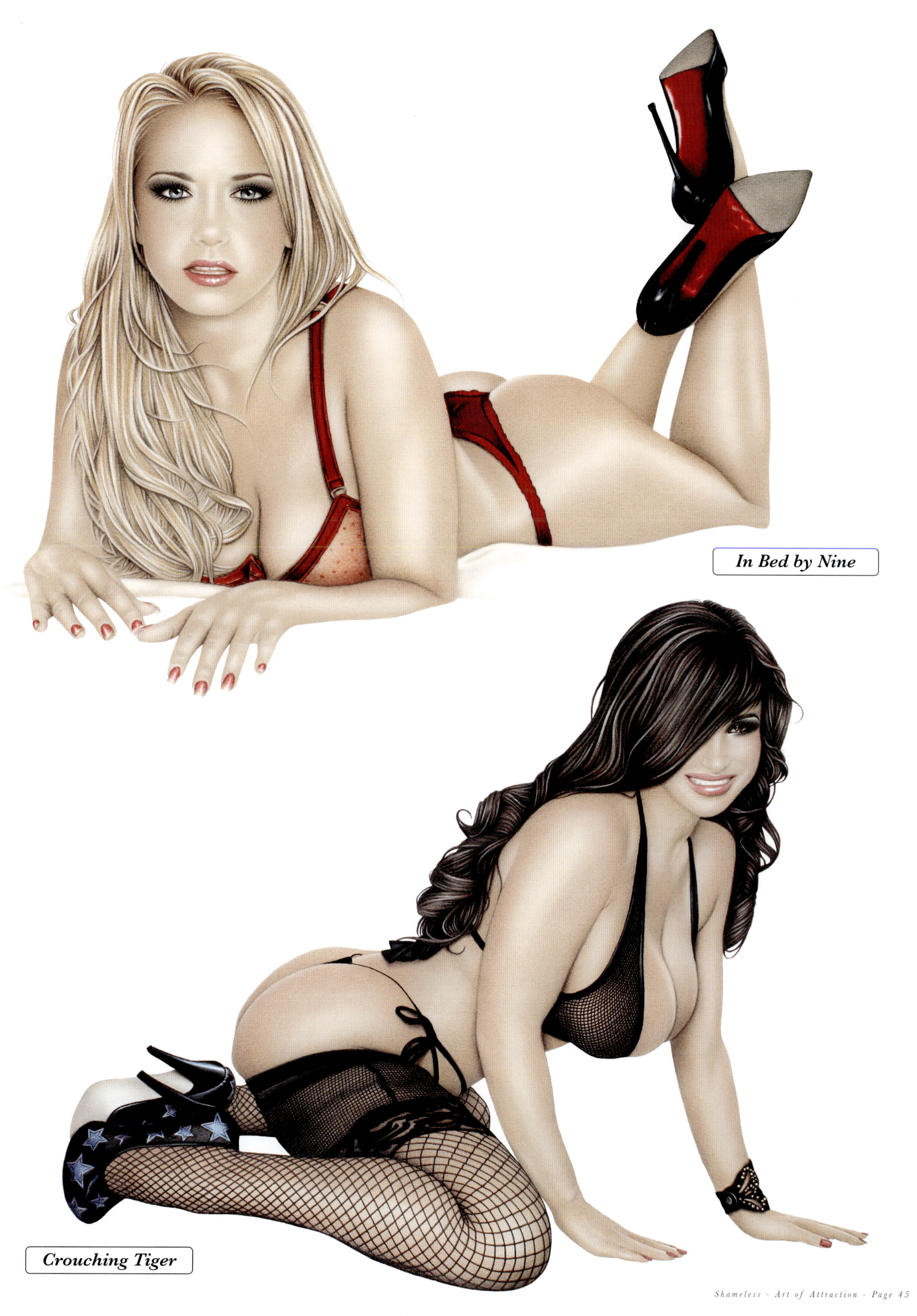

In Bed by Nine

Crouching Tiger

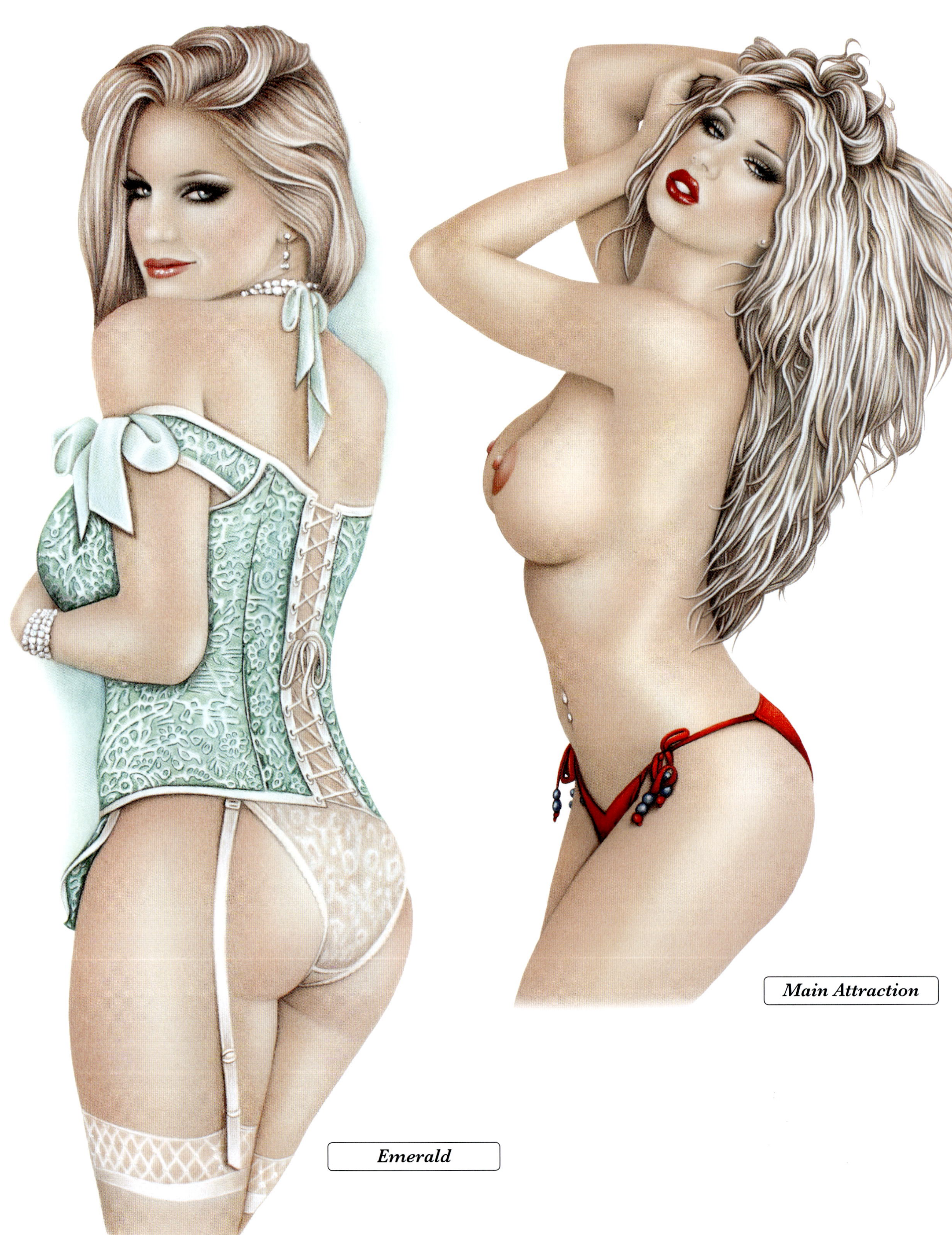

Emerald

Main Attraction

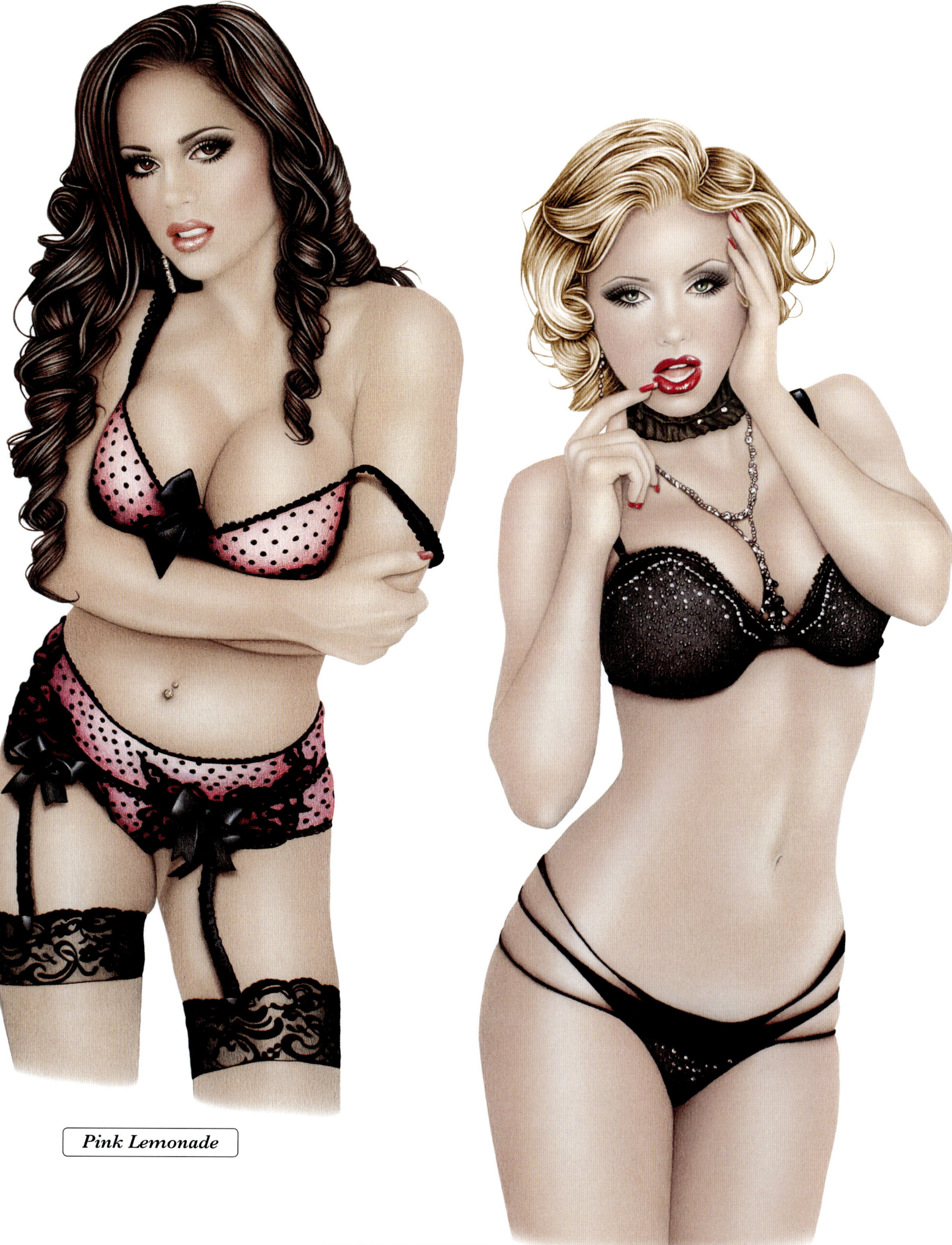

Pink Lemonade

Starlight

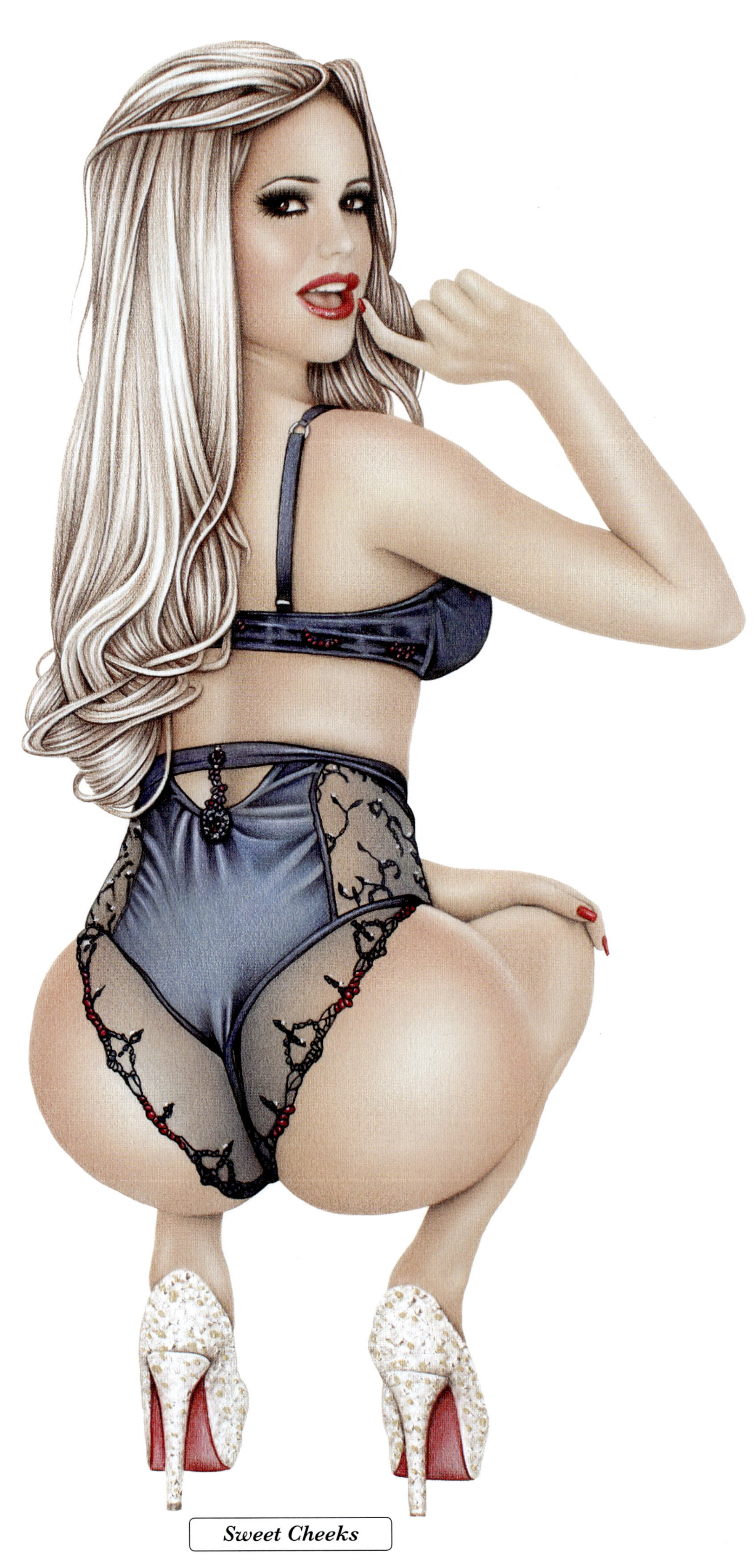

Sweet Cheeks